Hear Him

Hear Him

Listening to the Voice of God in Scriptures and in Our Lives

Taylor D. Halverson, Ph.D., and
Lisa R. Halverson, Ph.D.,
with Tyler J. Griffin, Ph.D.

ISBN 978-1-951341-13-8
Published by Line of Sight Publishing.
Cover image by Megan Lagerberg.
Cover design © 2020 by Megan Lagerberg, Taylor Halverson, and Lisa Halverson.
Typeset by Kathryn Jenkins.
Copyedited by Kathryn Jenkins.

Dedication

I dedicate this book to my parents, Richard Paul Halverson and Kathleen Taylor Ballstaedt Halverson, who showed me from a young age how to hear Him.

—TDH

To my parents, Mark Edmond Rampton and Alice Henderson Rampton. You have supported me through my own hearing struggles and my experience with deafness, and, more importantly, you have taught me the importance of listening to others and to God.

—LMRH

Dedicated to the opening of hearts everywhere to better hear Him.

—TJG

Table of Contents

Preface

ON FEBRUARY 26, 2020, God's chosen prophet for our time, President Russell M. Nelson, lovingly invited us with all the feeling of a tender parent to "think deeply and often about this key question: How do you hear Him?" President Nelson explained, "In the scriptures, there are very few sacred instances in which the voice of God the Father has been heard. So, when He says something, we really *need* to listen. Repeatedly, He has personally introduced His Beloved Son, Jesus Christ, with a specific charge to '*Hear Him!*'" President Nelson further encouraged us "to take steps to hear Him better and more often."

In his April 2020 general conference opening remarks, President Nelson urged us to "commence a lifelong quest to hear Him."

Later in that same conference, he instructed us further:

> When we seek to hear—truly hear—His Son, we will be guided to know what to do in any circumstance. The very first word in the Doctrine and Covenants is *hearken*. It means "to listen with the intent to obey." To hearken means to "hear Him"—to *hear* what

the Savior says and then to *heed* His counsel. In those two words—"Hear Him"—God gives us the pattern for success, happiness, and joy in this life. We are to *hear* the words of the Lord, *hearken* to them, and *heed* what He has told us! As we seek to be disciples of Jesus Christ, our efforts to *hear Him* need to be ever more intentional. It takes conscious and consistent effort to fill our daily lives with His words, His teachings, His truths.

To Hear Him, we should seek to be intentional, constant, consistent.

We have written this little book to inspire all of us to hear Him!

We hope this book helps all of us to be better at hearing the voice of God and acting on what we hear. We don't proclaim to have all the answers, for certainly each of us authors has struggled at times to recognize, hear, and act on the voice of God. But we've also seen in our personal lives and in the lives of untold faithful and faith-seeking children of God the transformative power of diligently seeking to feel the voice of God in our lives.

This book seeks to capture and highlight some of the instructive stories preserved in scripture about listening to and hearing God. We will also tell a few personal stories about hearing and deafness. And we'll explore each of the scriptural instances that preserve the voice of God the Father. Each section will include suggested activities, questions, or habits that will increase the likelihood of hearing God more often in our lives.

We are all children of God. He loves us with an unbreakable love. He hears us, and He wants us to hear Him!

The Art of Hearing God with Your Heart

By Tyler Griffin

NEPHI IS A POWERFUL WRITER, yet he worries about his weakness as a writer:

> And now I, Nephi, cannot write all the things which were taught among my people; neither am I mighty in writing, like unto speaking; for when a man speaketh by the power of the Holy Ghost the power of the Holy Ghost carrieth it unto the hearts of the children of men. (2 Nephi 33:1)

How many times have you read the books of 1 and 2 Nephi and thought to yourself, *Wow! This is so painful! Nephi is such a bad writer. I wish we could just listen to him speak, because it's so hard to work through his poor writing!* Probably never. If Nephi's writing ability is so amazing, we can only imagine what it would have been like to sit in an audience where he was *speaking,* based on what he told us in the verse quoted above.

Look at what he says: "when a man speaketh by the power of the Holy Ghost the power of the Holy Ghost carrieth it *unto* the hearts of the children of men" (emphasis added). Pay attention to that highlighted preposition. If a man or a woman is speaking by the power of the Holy Ghost, the power of the Holy Ghost carries it *unto* the hearts of the children of men. Nephi explains that if you are doing your job as a speaker, the power of the Holy Ghost will carry it **unto** the hearts of your listeners. The preposition we would have probably preferred that he used there would be *in* or *into*.

What's the only difference between those prepositions? You'll notice that it comes down to *U* (you) and *I*.

Let's play this out a little bit further. Pretend that I am a student in your class or sitting in a sacrament meeting where you are teaching or growing up as a child in your family. If you do your job as a teacher, speaker, or parent, you will have prepared by the power of the Holy Ghost. You will have done what is necessary to prepare your heart and your mind to deliver the right kind of information in the right way. You (or, using the play on words, *U*) will have done your part, and the Holy Ghost will respond by carrying that message **unto** my heart, but not necessarily *into* my heart.

Now let's share a fascinating little wordplay going on in English with the word *heart*. The first four letters are **hear**. Looking closer, you will notice that you have an **ear** right in the middle of your heart. It is enclosed, not on the wings. This means your heart must be softened and open in order to hear.

By the way, it is He (the first two letters of *heart*) to whom you really listen. Not mortals. Not the people at the pulpit. Not the people sitting around you. You listen to the voice of the Spirit.

Listening to and understanding His voice is somewhat of a he**ART** form.

Over time, listening with your full heart gets easier, just as with learning a foreign language. With time and practice you gain proficiency and fluency. The more you soften, and the more you ask God to soften and open your heart, the better that internal *ear* can hear. You will get to the point where even if the speaker or teacher is struggling and has not prepared, the Holy Ghost come can still come and teach you what you need to hear, because the most important truths you're going to ever learn in life aren't going to bounce off your eardrums. They will be truths that are felt deep in your heart. That is where your life changes—down in the heart.

People don't change because of things they only see or hear. They change because of truths they feel in their heart.

Back to 2 Nephi 33:1 and the question of U (you) and I fulfilling our different roles in the teaching and learning process. Nephi seems to be lamenting that he can't force his message *into* our hearts. He can't do my job for me as a learner. He masterfully fulfilled his role as a prophet and teacher. But even if he could speak to us today, the best that could happen is that his message would be carried *unto* our hearts. Now, for the rest of our lives, it is our turn to fulfill our role in this process to ensure that these messages sink increasingly deeper *into* our hearts.

CALL TO ACTION: Think of a time when you *knew* God was speaking to your heart. What led up to that experience? What did you do to invite the Lord to soften your heart and help you open it? List one way this week you can more fully open your heart to the Spirit of God.

Hearing the Voice of God the Father in Scripture

By Tyler Griffin

BEFORE ADAM AND EVE PARTOOK OF the fruit in the Garden of Eden and subsequently fell from the presence of God, Restoration sources indicate that Heavenly Father did most of the talking, most of the teaching, and most of the instructing. After Adam and Eve were expelled from the Garden of Eden, they no longer walked and talked with God the Father. They were not at-one with Him anymore. The word *at-one-ment* or *atonement* is the process or product whereby Jesus Christ brings us back to again be "at one" with God.

After the Fall, the voice of the Father doesn't seem to be the direct source of instruction and guidance for Adam and Eve and their posterity. They hear the voice of a mediator, a go-between, who acts as an intercessor between fallen mortals and God in His perfection.

We call upon God in the name of His Son, Jesus Christ. Additionally, we learn that the Savior's mediating role goes between us and God in both directions: "But God did call on men, in the name of his Son, (this being the plan of redemption which was laid) saying: If ye will repent, and harden not your hearts, then will I have mercy upon you, through mine Only Begotten Son" (Alma 12:33).

Jesus intercedes for us *and* for God. Jesus presents us to God. And Jesus presents God to us. When the Father speaks to fallen mortals in scriptures, His message seems to be focused on introducing and bearing witness of His Son. We come to know the Father through the Son. And we find our way back to God through the Son.

According to the scriptural record, it appears that almost everything after the Fall was delegated from the Father to the Son. This is the Church of Jesus Christ. We teach the gospel of Jesus Christ. The Book of Mormon is Another Testament of Jesus Christ. All these things were delegated to the Son to build up His kingdom so it could one day be presented spotless to the Father (see D&C 76:107). This delegation process began way back in the beginning, even while Adam and Eve were still in the garden. Right after partaking of the forbidden fruit, they clothed themselves in fig-leaf aprons to cover their newly discovered nakedness. God the Father then asked His Son Jesus Christ to prepare coats of skins for Adam and Eve. In that moment we see the symbolic baton being passed to Jesus. And interestingly, for the first time ever, Adam and Eve must watch animals die. They had never seen death before. And it was Jesus who was demonstrating this so that Adam and Eve would know how to perform these sacrifices—powerful symbols for the Savior's future infinite sacrifice.

But note that there are some things that the Father didn't delegate. Probably the first thing that comes to mind is prayer. Though we are in a fallen and mortal state, we still talk directly to the Father through Jesus or in the name of our mediator, the intercessor Jesus Christ. Prayer was not delegated to the Son. That was kept in the hands of God the Father.

Thankfully, we still have a direct line to Him in that regard. He doesn't speak quite as directly back. But He *does* speak through the Holy Ghost and through his Son. Hence the invitation to hear Him!

Nevertheless, there are a few rare instances where the voice of God the Father is recorded and preserved in scripture. Let's look at look at those cases and contemplate what doctrinal truths we can learn.

God the Father Introduces Jesus at His Baptism

The first time in scripture that we hear the voice of God the Father (outside of the Garden of Eden) is at the baptism of Christ. His statement in Matthew is very simple, very short, and very succinct: "This is my beloved Son, in whom I am well pleased" (Matthew 3:17).

That's it! God is introducing the group gathered at the Jordan River to His beloved Son.

Mark's and Luke's accounts are a little different, because the emphasis is on the Father talking directly to the Son.

> *"Thou art my beloved Son, in whom I am well pleased" (Mark 1:11).*

> *"Thou art my beloved Son; in thee I am well pleased" (Luke 3:22).*

What do we learn from this? God testifies of His Son. And God loves His Son.

God the Father Introduces Jesus on the Mount of Transfiguration

Later in Jesus's ministry, we hear the voice of the Father again when Jesus is on the Mount of Transfiguration with Peter, James, and John. A bright cloud overshadows them, and they hear a voice out of the cloud: "This is my beloved Son, in whom I am well pleased; hear ye him" (Matthew 17:5).

As at the baptismal scene, the only thing the Father does is introduce the Son with His true identity. This is significant. Peter, James, and John hear the voice of God the Father testifying of His Son.

God the Father Introduces Jesus in the Sacred Grove

In one of the segments of the video *Special Witnesses of Christ* filmed in the Sacred Grove in Palmyra, New York, President Gordon B. Hinckley taught a profound truth. As he stood in the Sacred Grove, he declared that it was in that location where the most powerful testimony of Jesus Christ was given in this dispensation. That most powerful testimony of Jesus Christ doesn't come from any mortal or any combination of mortals. It comes from God the Father Himself.

The Father and the Son were together in the garden before the Fall. But after the Fall, it wasn't until the First Vision in the Sacred Grove that the Father and Son came into the fallen world together. And what was the Father's message to Joseph? *"This is My Beloved Son. Hear Him!"* (Joseph Smith—History 1:17).

As President Hinckley explained, those eight words provide the single most powerful testimony given in our dispensation of Jesus Christ and of His divinity, because God Himself said in essence, "This is Him. Hear Him. Listen to Him." Nobody can bear a stronger testimony that Jesus is the Christ, the Son of God, than God Himself!

If that's the most powerful witness and testimony of Jesus Christ in our dispensation, then the most powerful testimonies that Jesus is the Christ in our New Testament record have to be at the baptism of Christ and the Mount of Transfiguration when God Himself speaks and people listen. No other testimony is more important than the Father saying, "This is my Beloved Son. Hear Him!"

God the Father Introduces Jesus to the Nephites

Now let's consider the only other major time where the voice of the Father introduces the Son: to the Nephites in Bountiful (see 3 Nephi 11:3–5). The Nephites who were gathered at the temple in Bountiful twice heard a voice, but they did not understand what they were hearing. Finally, the third time, they opened their ears to hear and they cast their eyes up towards the sound—and then they understood. In that New World context, God the Father gave a few more words than we read in biblical accounts. Specifically, God declared that Jesus was now glorified, a description we do not see in the New Testament accounts. But the main idea is the same. God expressed His love for His Son and commanded the people to hear Jesus: "Behold my Beloved Son, in whom I am well pleased, in whom I have glorified my name— hear ye him" (3 Nephi 11:7).

Other Times God the Father Spoke in Scripture (2 Nephi 31 and Helaman 5)

There are some additional instances of God the Father speaking that are often overlooked in scripture. One is in 2 Nephi 31:11: "And the Father said: Repent ye, repent ye, and be baptized in the name of my Beloved Son."

Immediately after the Father tells us all to be baptized in the name of the Son, what follows is significant. Nephi records what he learned from hearing the voice of the Son:

"He that is baptized in my name, to him will the Father give the Holy Ghost, like unto me; wherefore, follow me, and do the things which ye have seen me do" (2 Nephi 31:12).

A second time God the Father spoke is recorded in 2 Nephi 31:14–15. Notice again how Nephi is able to distinguish the differences between the voice of God the Father and the voice of God the Son!

> But, behold, my beloved brethren, *thus came the voice of the Son unto me, saying*: After ye have repented of your sins, and witnessed unto the Father that ye are willing to keep my commandments, by the baptism of water, and have received the baptism of fire and of the Holy Ghost, and can speak with a new tongue, yea, even with the tongue of angels, and after this should deny me, it would have been better for you that ye had not known me.
>
> *And I heard a voice from the Father, saying*: Yea, the words of my Beloved are true and faithful. He that endureth to the end, the same shall be saved. (Emphasis added)

The work of God the Father and God the Son is so simple, beautiful, and powerful. The Father and the Son both testify of each other and show us a perfect example of what it means to be *one*.

An additional place in 2 Nephi 31 where we hear the voice of the Father is in verse 20. In this verse, we learn what it means to really *Hear Him*—it means to feast upon His words.

> Wherefore, ye must press forward with a steadfastness in Christ, having a perfect brightness of hope, and a love of God and of all men. Wherefore, if ye shall press forward, feasting upon the word of Christ, and endure to the end, behold, *thus saith the Father*: Ye shall have eternal life. (Emphasis added)

No testifier is more powerful than God Himself. Nobody. He presides over everyone and everything. He is saying in humble simplicity, "If you will just do all of these things that my Son has told you to do, you will have eternal life."

There is one other significant scriptural location where we hear the voice of the Father— one that is often overlooked. In Helaman 5, Nephi and Lehi, sons of Helaman, go forth on a mission among the Lamanites in the Land of Nephi. The Lamanites cast them into prison. When their captors come to execute them, a shadow or a cloud descends and a deep fear shrouds the souls of their captors. In the darkness, everyone hears a voice, which is probably the voice of Jesus Christ, commanding them, "Repent ye, repent ye, and seek no more to destroy my servants whom I have sent unto you to declare good tidings" (Helaman 5:29).

Mormon goes on to describe the voice and the effect it had.

> And it came to pass when they heard this voice, and beheld that it was not a voice of thunder, neither was it a voice of a great tumultuous noise, but behold, it was a still voice of perfect mildness, as if it had been a whisper, and it did pierce even to the very soul—
>
> And notwithstanding the mildness of the voice, behold the earth shook exceedingly, and the walls of the prison trembled again, as if it were about to tumble to the earth; and behold the cloud of darkness, which had overshadowed them, did not disperse. (Helaman 5:30–31)

A third time the voice came uttering marvelous words. The Lamanites could not flee because of the overpowering darkness. But there was a Nephite dissenter among them named Aminadab who turned to see Nephi and Lehi staring up into heaven. The Lamanites who were with him asked what they should do to be released from the darkness. Aminadab explained, "You must repent, and cry unto the voice, even until ye shall have faith in Christ, who was taught unto you by Alma, and Amulek, and Zeezrom; and when ye shall do this, the cloud of darkness shall be removed from overshadowing you" (Helaman 5:41). In essence, Aminadab was inviting them to *hear Him.*

The Lamanites did hear the voice of the Son, and they responded appropriately. They cried to God for deliverance. As they did, they beheld that they were encircled about by fire, experiencing no harm. The Holy Ghost descended from heaven and entered their hearts.

Then they heard the voice of God the Father. Notice the similar descriptions between His voice and the voice of His Son in verses 30–31:

> And it came to pass that there came a voice unto them, yea, a pleasant voice, as if it were a whisper, saying: Peace, peace be unto you, because of your faith in my Well Beloved, who was from the foundation of the world. (Helaman 5:46–47)

To really hear the voice of God, we must be still. The voice of the Father *wasn't* yelling at them. His voice was not punishing. His voice was a pleasant voice as if it were a whisper. And it was delivering peace because they had listened to the voice of the Son. The message is simple and sweet. God the Father testifies, in essence, "Because you have listened to my Son, you will have peace."

It seems that the most often-repeated word in scriptures revealing the voice of the Father to mortals is the word *beloved.* Jesus Christ knows that Heavenly Father loves Him. But oh, how it must make Him feel to hear the Father expressing that love over and over. One significant lesson here is that if we want to become more like our Heavenly Father, we ought to do a better job of *expressing* our love for others rather than just *feeling* love for them. God the Father perfectly and beautifully expresses perfect love.

Jesus Christ wants to save us. He's willing to forgive us if we'll just trust Him and come unto Him. As we *hear Him,* we will increasingly understand and be able to live the laws and commandments of His everlasting gospel. We will find peace. That peace in Christ will, in due time, lead us to the Father. In fact, Jesus's whole mission was not to bring us to Him as the end goal. His mission is not complete until He has prepared us sufficiently to the point where He can present us spotless before the Father.

CALL TO ACTION: Record a time in your life when you more fully heard the voice of God the Father because you followed the Son. Consider sharing your experience with others.

Losing My Hearing and Gaining a Sure Knowledge of God

By Lisa Halverson

LAST YEAR I BECAME 100 percent, totally deaf. The loss of all natural sound, the reliance on assistive devices to hear and comprehend, and the experience of struggling to hear those around me has increased the importance and relevance to me of scriptures about hearing the voice of the Lord.

My ability to hear natural sound has always been compromised. I was born with a mild hearing loss; it slowly worsened, but technology simultaneously advanced in incredible ways. By my junior year at Stanford University, I got my first pair of hearing aids. As my loss advanced from "mild" to "moderate" to "severe," I relied more and more on those aids to allow me to hear and comprehend human speech. I was grateful for technology and assumed it would allow me to hear until scientists eventually discovered how to regrow the sensorineural nerve endings that enable hearing.

Then four years ago my left ear suffered a catastrophic decline, decimating comprehension through that ear. I qualified for my first cochlear implant. Despite what touching YouTube videos depict, most cochlear recipients do not comprehend speech upon "activation." Instead it can take months and even years to turn electrical impulses into understandable sound. My brain adapted slowly; only after three years did I both comprehend well *and* stop gritting my teeth at the quality of sound received through my cochlear.

During those same three years during which I was working to regain comprehension through a cochlear in my left ear, hearing in my right ear flickered in and out. It plummeted once, then twice—but both times advancements in treatment restored much of the new loss. With one cochlear whose quality I still did not like, I was terrified of losing hearing in the second ear—and with it, losing all natural sound. No longer recognizing my husband's voice. Never knowing what my son's voice would sound like after puberty hit and it first cracked. No longer discerning between my daughter's laugh and her cry. Never hearing a grandbaby's gurgle. I sobbed into my pillow at night for these losses and potential losses. It was only after a powerful experience with the Spirit gave me a sure knowledge of the reality of the resurrection that I was able to say, "Thy will be done."

When hearing in the right ear crashed to zero a year ago and did not respond to treatment, the moment I had been fearing arrived: I lost all access to natural sound. Fortunately, my brain had finally adapted to the cochlear implant in my left ear, and speech sounded decently normal and natural through it. But being binaural (hearing with both ears) is important for directionality and for comprehending with background noise. So even though I didn't want to go under the surgical knife again, I plunged in and received a second cochlear implant.

Almost a year later, my brain is still adapting. To understand and interpret sound, I rely on the older "good" cochlear implant, the novice cochlear implant, environmental awareness, and lots of speechreading (the more correct term for what is often called "lip reading," because it involves not only watching lips but also paying attention to body language, context, and facial expressions).

Hearing loss has made me a very skilled and dedicated *listener*. I wish I could say that is has also made me amazingly attuned to spiritually hearing the voice of the Lord, but I still have a long way to go. Hearing loss *has* piqued my interest in studying hearing and listening as themes in scriptures. Here are a few core themes I have noticed.

The Key Differences between Hearing and Understanding

One thing you realize when you are deaf or hard of hearing is the significant difference between *hearing* and *listening*. One who has normal hearing *hears* without much effort.

Even *I* hear quite a bit of sound through my cochlear implants—it just doesn't always make meaningful sense. Hearing is easy!

But *listening*, and the *understanding* that comes from it, is hard work. Listening requires time and focus and empathy and the ability to be more intent on the other person than on our own next response. The Lord does not want us to only *hear* His word, but to *listen* to it intently, to *understand* His meaning, and to *obey* His guidance.

Sometimes I have treated the receipt of revelation as if it should be as effortless as hearing sound is for those with perfect hearing. But receiving revelation is an exercise not in hearing but in understanding meaning. That requires preparation and work. That requires listening.

Preparing the "Acoustics"

I do a *lot* of work to ensure that I understand the people around me. There are some situations where I just can't win: group conversations in a noisy environment, for example, are just about impossible for me. However, if my husband and I go out to eat at a restaurant, I can bring along a "mini mic" to prioritize his voice above all the other chaos. When my children speak, I try to come close and face them and to use my speechreading as well as my listening skills. I ask them to take turns, since for me, competing and concurrent voices become noise, not speech. I arrive at meetings early and grab a seat in the front row, and even then I crane my neck to see speakers and incline my body to catch everything being said. Every night I recharge the device batteries so that I can hear and understand the following day.

Do I make the same efforts to "prepare the acoustics" when listening to God? Do I take time to listen to Him before I jump into the "noisy environments" of daily life? Do I prioritize His voice over the chaos that surrounds me? Do I really come close and face Him with my full attention? Do I find a spiritual "mini mic" so that I can prioritize the voice of God? Do I recharge physically and spiritually so I can understand new communication every day? Finally, is He on *my* front row? Am I inclining my ear (see D&C 121:4) to hear Him? I know I can do better. If I work that hard to hear the noise of the world, can I work a little harder to hear the inspiration of the heavens?

Listening to God Builds Our Relationship with Him and Allows Us to Become Like Him

Helen Keller, who was both deaf and blind, purportedly said, "Blindness cuts us off from things, but deafness cuts us off from people." Conversely, careful listening draws us close to others, strengthening and deepening our relationships. A baby grows to know its mother's voice while in the womb, unable yet to see her face. Through listening to the voice of the mother, the baby comes to trust the sound and the person behind that sound.

Listening does the same thing for our relationship with God. Think of this life as a womb preparing each of us, spirit and flesh together as a soul, for all that God knows we are capable of. Although there is a veil of darkness in this "womb" and we cannot at this time see everything that lies ahead, we can grow as we listen for and obey the Lord's voice. Like the baby in the womb, we do not see Him at this time, but by listening we can come to trust Him. But if we choose not to listen to His voice, we are choosing spiritual deafness to accompany our temporary, veiled blindness.

Fortunately, spiritual deafness does not require expensive hearing aids or invasive cochlear implants to resolve; it requires "a broken heart and a contrite spirit" (3 Nephi 9:20). *Those* are the only "assistive hearing devices" that we need—and the quality of sound they provide is pitch perfect! But just as with the cochlear, it may take months and even years—nay, a lifetime—of practice for us to hear and understand with progressively better clarity and quality.

One day I *will* stand before the Lord and, I hope, "be like him" and, veil lifted, "see him as he is" (Moroni 7:48). To recognize and be like Him on that great day, it will be absolutely necessary to have spent my life hearkening to His voice. Seeing Him will be bittersweet, I think, if spiritual deafness means I cannot even understand His voice.

Seeing the Lord Is Not Enough

I do yearn for the day I will see Him face to face. The scriptures give stunning examples of those who have the resplendent experience of seeing the Lord or His messengers in this life. The brother of Jared saw the Lord's finger and then, through faith, His entire being (see Ether 3:6–16). Lehi beheld visions of God and Jesus Christ (see 1 Nephi 1:8–9), and Nephi and Jacob saw their Redeemer (see 2 Nephi 11:2–3). Abish was "converted unto the Lord . . . on account of a remarkable vision of her father" (Alma 19:16). Joseph entered a grove of trees and beheld the "First Vision" of God the Father and His Son (see JS—H 1:17). Mary Whitmer saw the angel Moroni and the gold plates (*Saints*, 1:70–71). Stalwart action followed each of these remarkable visions of God and His messengers.

Yet there are numerous instances where visions do *not* lead to changes in action. Laman and Lemuel saw an angel of the Lord, but they listened not to the Spirit, and their hearts were not permanently changed.

I propose that even though these astounding visions may seem the zenith of spiritual interaction with God, the vision is not what brings us close to God. That happens through hearkening unto His voice.

Let me relate this to a story from my (lack of!) hearing experience. When my husband was in graduate school at Indiana University-Bloomington, I joined a support group led by one of the professors of audiology, who himself had a mild hearing loss. One night we spoke about speechreading. All of us felt we were excellent speechreaders. We all found it very important to be able to "read" faces and see expressions as we listened. For example, my comprehension in my new cochlear *doubles* when I can watch the face of the speaker. Despite our confidence in our speechreading abilities, when we tried to tell what was being said in a video with the sound turned off, we failed dismally.

Similarly, sight alone falls short of giving one an understanding of God. Throughout the scriptures, hearkening to the voice of the Lord is crucial to real understanding and the real change that can follow it. Listening to God is our primary means of experiencing Him during this life!

God Is Moved to Act on Our Behalf when He Listens to Us!

Listening is one way God shows us His love. We are always before His all-seeing eye. But I have also been struck by the number of scriptures describing how He is moved when He hears our cries. I love these words describing the Savior from Alma 9:26—

- full of grace, equity, and truth,
- full of patience, mercy, and long-suffering,
- quick to *hear* the cries of his people
- and to answer their prayers.

If we approach Him with love and humility, He will respond quickly to our cries. He yearns to hear us, just as we yearn to hear Him. I am so grateful that this type of communication can never be compromised by a physical limitation.

CALL TO ACTION: What "limitations" have you experienced in your life that can actually help you better hear God and feel His love?

Hearing the Voice of God Leads to Creation

By Taylor Halverson

ACCORDING TO THE OLD TESTAMENT, one of God's very first acts of creation was to speak. At the voice of God, creation emerged from watery chaos: "And God said, Let there be light: and there was light" (Genesis 1:3). The elements heard the voice of God and obeyed. Light burst forth throughout the universe. God spoke, and because the elements listened to His voice, order came to creation. And it was good: "And God saw the light, that it was good" (Genesis 1:4).

Are our lives ever disordered? Chaotic? Confused? Lacking light or purpose? The Creation story demonstrates that God comes to create order. He separates opposites, puts everything into its proper relationship, sets its bounds, and by establishing order brings creation. When we hear His voice, we can have the chaotic darkness of our lives banished to its appointed realm. We can see the light of God shining forth in darkness.

We are part of God's created order. We can learn from observing His other creations that hearing and immediately obeying the voice of God leads to goodness. If we seek to taste goodness in our lives, we can experience it as we obediently listen to the voice of God as He creates our beautiful forevers.

God is purposeful in creating. He has a plan. He seeks to save His children. He put into place the Creation so that we could have a stage for experiencing His salvation. We wonder at the joy the elements must feel knowing that as they obey God, they help support the conditions for us to experience the plan of salvation.

CALL TO ACTION: As you see and experience the beauties of God's creation, how do you hear the voice of God?

Adam and Eve Hide from the Voice of God

By Taylor Halverson

ADAM AND EVE WERE THE first humans to fully experience the beauties of God's created order. In the Garden of Eden, God had prepared for their every need to be met. He gave simple instructions to our first parents about the garden, directing them "to dress it and to keep it" (Genesis 2:10). The Hebrew word used here for "dress it" could more properly be translated as "serve in the garden." The Hebrew word for "keep it" also means to "guard, protect, and observe the garden."

We later see in the story that after God removed Adam and Eve from the garden, He placed Cherubim and a flaming sword to "keep it"—that is, to "guard" the way back into the garden and protect the garden from any unauthorized entering. The Cherubim ended up performing the task God assigned to Adam and Eve after they failed to do what they heard from the voice of God.

Satan came among them, tempting them, confusing them, and teaching them truth mixed with falsehood. Adam and Eve chose to hear and heed the voice of Satan instead of the voice of God. Immediately they recognized their transgression and felt shame.

Then they heard the voice of God.

And *they heard the voice of the LORD God* walking in the garden in the cool of the day: and Adam and his wife hid themselves from the presence of the LORD God amongst the trees of the garden. (Genesis 3:8; emphasis added)

Instead of the joy that God intends for those who *hear* and *obey* His voice, Adam and Eve experienced what we have all tasted—the disappointment of not living up to our blessings and God's magnificent expectations of us. Adam and Eve responded the way humans commonly do when we have done something wrong. We hide and wish that the rocks and mountains could keep God's all-piercing eye from finding us.

Who among us hasn't felt as Adam—naked or exposed when we've done something wrong and God asks us to account? "I heard thy voice in the garden, and I was afraid, because I was naked; and I hid myself" (Genesis 3:12).

We all have times when we hear the voice of God and recognize our own nothingness before Him. We may feel to hide from our Creator, the Father of our souls. But when we follow Adam and Eve's example of hearing God and acknowledging our nothingness before Him, we will ultimately receive the blessings of His never-ending forgiveness that leads to joy and spiritual growth:

[Adam   declared]   because   of my transgression my eyes are opened, and in this life I shall have joy, and again in the flesh I shall see God. And Eve, his wife, heard all these things and was glad, saying: Were it not for our transgression we never should have had seed, and never should have known good and evil, and the joy of our redemption, and the eternal life which God giveth unto all the obedient. And Adam and Eve blessed the name of God, and they made all things known unto their sons and their daughters. (Moses 5:10–12)

As children of God, and as children of Adam and Eve, we have the promise of eternal life if we learn to heed the voice of God.

CALL TO ACTION: What have you heard from God that has made you glad? How have you blessed God because of Him hearing you?

Hagar and Ishmael Hear God Who Heard Their Cries

By Taylor Halverson

HEARING GOD IS NOT A one-way street with God doing all the talking and us doing all the listening. God also hears us. In Genesis 16 and Genesis 21, we find two interrelated and often-overlooked Bible stories that exemplify the principle of hearing God and that also provide examples of God hearing His children. Both stories focus on Hagar and Ishmael. Hagar was Sarah's handmaiden, and Ishmael was Abraham's firstborn son.

These stories are part of the Abraham Cycle, the series of stories contained in Genesis 12–25 that track the life of Abraham. Remember that in Genesis 12 God came to Abraham and gave Him the spectacular promises of posterity, property, and prosperity (incidentally, the best meaning of *prosper* is to "have God's presence with us"). Those promises are available to all of Abraham's children, whether by blood or adoption. One of the purposes of the Restoration is to bring together all of God's children to receive the Abrahamic promises.

In Genesis 16, after Hagar became pregnant, Sarah felt jealous and cast Hagar out into the wilderness. There the Lord found Hagar and encouraged her to return to Sarah at Abraham's tent. Then the Lord delivered this astonishing promise to Hagar: "I will multiply thy seed exceedingly, that it shall not be numbered for multitude" (Genesis 16:10). Hagar heard and received directly from God a promise like what Abraham received. Incidentally, when you see the Old Testament phrase *the angel of the Lord*, know that this is one of the ways that the prophetic writers spoke of God in reverential tones.

Further, "The angel of the LORD said unto [Hagar], Behold, thou art with child, and shalt bear a son, and shalt *call his name Ishmael*; because the *LORD hath heard* thy affliction" (Genesis 16:11; emphasis added). Here is a hidden gem in the Hagar story. Ishmael's name in Hebrew literally means "God hears!" (*Ishm* = "hear," *El or Elohim* = "God"). Tucked inside this often-overlooked story of loss and redemption is a Hebrew word play that teaches us the powerful principle of hearing the voice of God.

Genesis 21 is similar to Genesis 16. After Abraham and Sarah's promised son Isaac was born, Sarah worried about Ishmael taking Isaac's inheritance. So Sarah sent Hagar and Ishmael away from the family. Hagar and Ishmael wandered in the wilderness. As their water and food depleted, they began to starve to death in the wilderness. As Hagar contemplated their sad state, worrying that her son would die, "She said, Let me not see the death of the child . . . and lift up her voice, and wept" (Genesis 21:16).

God heard!

We next see what at first seems unexpected. God made stunning promises to Ishmael. We may wonder why until we remember that as a child of Abraham, Ishmael received and had access to all the promises of Abraham. And faithful Hagar, as a wife within the covenant, also had full access to the Abrahamic promises. God heard the heartfelt cry of His daughter and son:

> And *God heard* the voice of the lad; and the angel of God called to Hagar out of heaven, and said unto her, What aileth thee, Hagar? fear not; for God hath *heard the voice of the lad* where he is.
>
> Arise, lift up the lad, and hold him in thine hand; for I will make him a great nation. (Genesis 21:17–18; emphasis added)

What is the principle of this story? God hears us in our distress and our affliction. And we, too, can hear Him. When we do, we will hear His assurances and promises to us as children of the covenant and as a child of God.

CALL TO ACTION: When has God heard you in your distress and affliction?

Abraham Hears the Voice of God and the Promised Nation Is Saved

By Taylor Halverson

THE HIGH POINT OF THE Abraham stories (as found in Genesis 12–25) is probably Genesis 22—the binding of Isaac. After a lifetime of hearing the voice of God and fully trusting that God will always keep His promises, Abraham heard the voice of God yet again, but this time asking Him to do the unthinkable:

> And it came to pass after these things [what things? A lifetime of trials and tests that God had placed on his path to help Abraham develop trust in God], that God did [test] Abraham, and said unto him, Abraham: and [Abraham, hearing the voice of God,] said, Behold, here I am.
>
> And [God] said, Take now thy son, thine only son Isaac, whom thou lovest, and get thee into the land of Moriah; and offer him there for a burnt offering upon one of the mountains which I will tell thee of. (Genesis 22:1–2)

What searing thoughts must have surged through Abraham's heart! After decades of patiently waiting for the promised child, God now demanded that the child be returned. How would Abraham respond to hearing the voice of God? Would he stall for time? Would he delay? Would he flee from God's voice as Jonah had attempted?

Abraham, stalwart Abraham, *"rose up early in the morning, . . .* and took . . . Isaac his son, and clave the wood for the burnt offering, and rose up, and went unto the place of which God had told him" (Genesis 22:3; emphasis added). So trusting, so faithful was Father Abraham at hearing the voice of God that he made no delay. When others may sleep in or add to their chore chart to avoid the call of God, Abraham responded by hearing and immediately obeying at first opportunity.

Abraham remained alert with his sensitive ear and heart to hearing the voice of God. At the very moment that

> Abraham stretched forth his hand, and took the knife to slay his son.
>
> And the angel of the LORD called unto him out of heaven, and said, Abraham, Abraham: and he said, Here am I.
>
> And he said, Lay not thine hand upon the lad, neither do thou any thing unto him: for now I know that

thou fearest God, seeing thou hast not withheld thy son, thine only son from me. (Genesis 22:10–12)

Because Abraham heard God and obeyed *immediately* both times, his son was saved, a nation of posterity was preserved, and God's covenantal blessings were eternally secured.

CALL TO ACTION: Have you ever been confused when hearing the voice of God? What did you eventually learn? What did God eventually reveal to you?

Israelite Women Do Not Hearken to the Unethical Demands of Immoral Leaders

By Taylor Halverson

WHEN WE RECALL THE ISRAELITE story, we often highlight Abraham and Moses, as we do in this book, but we may miss the powerful story of hearkening to God exemplified by the noble Israelite women during Egyptian bondage. As a note, *hearkening* contains in its meaning the sense of listening *and* obeying.

After Joseph died, a new Pharaoh arose who knew not Joseph and believed that the Israelites, as foreigners in the land, were a threat instead of an asset. Seeking to curb the blessed population growth the Israelites were experiencing, the king of Egypt made an immoral and unethical demand of the Israelite midwives. Listen in to see how Shiphrah and Puah responded to the opportunity to hear and hearken to the Pharaoh:

And the king of Egypt spake to the Hebrew midwives, of which the name of the one was Shiphrah, and the name of the other Puah:

And he said, When ye do the office of a midwife to the Hebrew women, and see them upon the stools; if it be a son, then ye shall kill him: but if it be a daughter, then she shall live.

But the midwives feared [i.e., respected and listened to] God, and *did not as the king of Egypt commanded them,* but saved the men children alive. (Exodus 1:15–17; emphasis added)

These faithful Israelite women hearkened to their real and true leader, God. They did not turn away from all that was "honest, true, chaste, benevolent, [and] virtuous, [or from] . . . doing good" (Articles of Faith 13). They rejected the immoral demands of a fear-mongering leader. They demonstrated that when we hearken to God, we may have to risk our lives and livelihoods.

The sacrifice, the hearkening to God that these Israelite women exhibited, led to the salvation of Moses, who was the instrument of salvation God sent to the Israelites to save them from bondage.

CALL TO ACTION: What have you learned from hearkening to the voice of God in the face of contrary voices in the world?

Moses Hearing God unto Salvation

By Taylor Halverson

THE STORY OF MOSES IN the Bible is pivotal to the story of salvation. After years of groaning servitude in Egyptian bondage, God *heard* the cries of His people: "And God heard their groaning, and God remembered his covenant with Abraham, with Isaac, and with Jacob" (Exodus 2:24).

What is the covenant that God remembered? God remembered His promises, first delivered to Abraham in Genesis 12, to grant him a large and growing posterity that would bless the entire world, property where the covenant could be secured, and prosperity (that is, God's presence) to experience the covenant. God heard His people and was ready to act on His covenantal commitments.

The story of Moses is full of the theme of hearing God.

While Moses was tending the sheep of his father-in-law, Jethro, "*God called unto him* out of the midst of the bush, and said, Moses, Moses. And he said, Here am I" (Exodus 3:4; emphasis added). Moses *heard* God and immediately responded. There is much to learn from Moses on this point. Still, Moses was human. He felt his own inadequacies, his own real and perceived deficiencies. Moses had limiting fear, asking himself, "Who am I, that I should go unto Pharaoh, and that I should bring forth the children of Israel out of Egypt?" (Exodus 3:11).

Who among us has not felt as Moses—that when we hear the voice of God so personally and intimately in our lives we wonder, "Who am I that God would speak to me? To ask me to do some deed that stretches my faith and experience?" God gently replied to Moses and to all of us when we feel the ever-so-real self-doubt and self-questioning, "I will be with thee" (Exodus 3:12). Do we hear that? God has promised to be with us! When we choose to believe Him, we will hear Him and have His presence in our lives.

Even after Moses heard God's reassuring promise to be with him, Moses was still concerned the people of Israel would not hearken to him: "But, behold, *they [the children of Israel] will not believe me, nor hearken unto my voice:* for they will say, The LORD hath not appeared unto thee" (Exodus 4:1; emphasis added).

God then revealed to Moses His plan to do mighty signs and wonders among the children of Israel and the Egyptians so that there would be no question who was in power. But even though Moses heard God's plan, Moses also listened to his limiting fears, which kept him from fully listening to God. He heard—or imagined in his mind—the possible complaints and criticism he would receive from the children of Israel and the Egyptians. "And Moses said unto the LORD, O my Lord, I am not eloquent, neither heretofore, nor since thou hast spoken unto thy servant: but I am slow of speech, and of a slow tongue" (Exodus 4:10; emphasis added).

Again, God patiently taught Moses to trust Him:

And the LORD said unto him, Who hath made man's mouth? or who maketh the dumb, or deaf, or the seeing, or the blind? have not I the LORD?

Now therefore go, and *I will be with thy mouth, and teach thee what thou shalt say.* (Exodus 4:11–12; emphasis added)

What happened when Moses declared God's salvation to the Israelites? Did the bad and terrible things Moses imagined come to pass? Did the people laugh at him and reject him? No. "When [the children of Israel] *heard* that the LORD had visited the children of Israel, and that he had looked upon their affliction,

then they bowed their heads and worshipped"
(Exodus 4:31; emphasis added).

The people of Israel heard the word of the
Lord and received it with gladness.

But what of the Egyptians?

In contrast to the humble hearing of the
voice of God demonstrated by Moses and the
children of Israel, Pharaoh and the Egyptians
provide an opposite example. They did not
listen. They did not hear the voice of God. They
refused to understand. They stood in the way
of God's efforts, so God effected His plan to
save the Israelites with a mighty hand and with
signs and wonders.

Listen to this initial exchange between
Moses and Pharaoh; even after this initial
exchange, Pharaoh never did choose to hear
the voice of God:

> And afterward Moses and Aaron
> went in, and *told* Pharaoh, *Thus saith
> the LORD God of Israel,* Let my people
> go, that they may hold a feast unto me
> in the wilderness.
>
> And Pharaoh said, *Who is the
> LORD, that I should obey his voice* to
> let Israel go? I know not the LORD,
> neither will I let Israel go. (Exodus
> 5:1–2; emphasis added)

Look at the contrast. On one side, the
prophet of God is speaking on behalf of God,

giving an opportunity to *hear the voice of God*. On the other side is a symbol of the vainness, foolishness, and frailties of men who think that when they are learned or have power or education or prestige or wealth or position they have no need to hearken to the voice of God (see 2 Nephi 9:28). Pharaoh represents the very worst: those who purposely choose to be ignorant of the Lord and therefore close their ears to Him. If we question who God is, if we question His reality, if we wonder at His identity as did Pharaoh, can we hear and obey His voice? No, never.

The story of Israelite salvation reaches its climax at Mount Sinai, the sacred covenantal mountain. God brought the Israelites to Mount Sinai that they might hear His voice—but not just hear but *hearken and obey* that they might become His peculiar and special treasure:

> Now therefore, *if ye will obey my voice indeed,* and keep my covenant, then ye shall be a peculiar treasure unto me above all people: for all the earth is mine:
> And ye shall be unto me a kingdom of priests, and an holy nation. (Exodus 19:5–6; emphasis added)

Moses taught the people the commandments of God, and they demonstrated that they had indeed *heard God* and that they would *hearken to God*: "And all the people answered together, and said, *All that the Lord hath spoken we will do*" (Exodus 19:8). In essence, the people of Israel entered into a sacred covenant to be God's people by living by all the words that He had revealed or would reveal.

We weekly re-enact the ancient covenant at Sinai to hear and obey God when we partake of the sacrament and promise that we "are willing to take upon [us] the name of thy Son, and always remember him and keep his commandments which he has given them; that [we] may always have his Spirit to be with [us]" (D&C 20:77).

CALL TO ACTION: What covenantal blessings have you received from hearkening to the voice of God?

Rejecting the Voice of God Leads to Mourning and Misery

By Taylor Halverson

THE SPIRIT WAS WILLING, BUT the flesh was weak. Even though the Israelites promised God that they would be His treasured and chosen people, they began squabbling and complaining as if on a long family road trip gone bad. In fact, the ancient wilderness Israelites were so fickle and inconstant to God, they created a fake god for themselves. They produced a golden calf to *replace* God after Moses tarried for many days in the holy mountain receiving revelation (see Exodus 32). Only Moses's intervention kept God from permanently banning His people from the promised land. But as a whole, the Israelites had still not learned to hear and hearken to God. They were so full of fear, so full of doubt, so full of distraction.

After the twelve spies returned from traversing the breadth and depth of the promised land and brought incredible tales of a land rich and abundant with everything one could ever desire, ten of the spies dropped a bomb of doubt and fear upon the Israelite congregation (see

Numbers 13). They described in wild terms the gigantic size and overpopulated nature of the land. Only two spies—Caleb and Joshua—remained faithful to God. Because of the fear-mongering report from the ten spies, most of the Israelites turned against Moses and God.

At this point, God was no longer willing to bring His people to the promised land. They would not hear Him. They would not believe Him. They would not trust Him. So instead He let them wander for nearly forty years in the wilderness, telling them that only their children would be able to enter into the promised land (see Numbers 14):

> Because all those men which have seen my glory, and my miracles, which I did in Egypt and in the wilderness, and have tempted me now these ten times, *and [they] have not hearkened to my voice;*
> *Surely they shall not see the land* which I sware unto their fathers, neither shall any of them that provoked me see it. (Numbers 14:22–23; emphasis added)

What was the sad response of these stubborn, hard-hearted people? "And Moses told these sayings unto all the children of Israel: and *the people mourned greatly*" (Numbers 14:39; emphasis added).

God wants us to return to His presence. It is as easy and as simple as listening to His voice—as simple as casting eyes on the staff Moses raised in the wilderness to heal those bitten by snakes (see Numbers 21). But how many of the ancient Israelites refused to look, thinking the way was too simple? Similarly, how many of the Israelites refused to hear God when they had the witness of all His miraculous deeds in Egypt and the daily ongoing salvation He gave them in the wilderness? Because their ears were thick, because they turned away from hearkening to God, they lost what God had made possible.

These stories are preserved in the Bible as warning instruction for us. Will we choose to live in fear and miss God's saving voice? Will we live in carnal security, thus avoiding seeing God's saving hand in our lives? Or will we choose to be faithful to God? To be His chosen people by seeking His will? To learn from practice and ongoing effort to experience God's revelatory voice in our lives?

Let modern-day Israel follow the latter-day prophets to not only hear the voice of God but also heed His loving words.

CALL TO ACTION: Have God or His servants ever asked you to do something difficult or to exercise considerable faith? What did you learn from that experience?

Hear, O Israel! The Ancient Israelite Article of Faith

By Taylor Halverson

AFTER FORTY DIFFICULT YEARS OF wandering and testing in the wilderness, the Israelites were ready to be brought by God into the promised land. But He had some additional covenantal instructions to share with them before they crossed over the River Jordan. God revealed through Moses the book of Deuteronomy, which literally means "second law" or "second telling of the law." The book of Deuteronomy summarizes, expands, and clarifies the covenantal promises and instructions first delivered to the Israelites at Mount Sinai (see Exodus 19–23).

One of the revelations established by God in Deuteronomy is what we might call an ancient Israelite article of faith: "Hear, O Israel: The Lord our God is one Lord" (Deuteronomy 6:4).

Hearing is first. Hearing is the alpha. God's words are the omega. Where there is no listening, where there is no hearing the voice of God, His words effectively do not exist for the spiritually deaf. Without first hearkening to God's command to hear, we cannot live the commandments He reveals. Without first hearing God, we cannot know of the promised joys He has prepared for the faithful Saints. Who can know of any of the revelations or words of God if they do not *first hear*?

So fundamental is this ancient Israelite article of faith throughout Israelite history and religion that even today Jews tack a small inscribed container with a small scroll carefully tucked inside at the entrance of each door. The outward-facing inscription is a single Hebrew letter derived from the first letter of the Hebrew word for "hearing." As Jews enter and exit doors, which are symbolic transition places, they are constantly reminded that in all their comings and goings, they are first and foremost commanded to hear!

This ancient article of faith is as true and necessary as it was when God first revealed it millennia ago.

CALL TO ACTION: How do you remember to hear the voice of God? What visual cues can you put into your everyday environment to remind you to hear the voice of God?

Hannah Experiences God's Grace Hearing Her at His Tabernacle

By Taylor Halverson

MANY GENERATIONS AFTER THE ISRAELITES had been secured in the land of promise by the power of God, an otherwise nondescript, unknown Israelite woman journeyed on a religious pilgrimage to the mobile holy spot of God's presence called the tabernacle. Her heart was full of faith and full of pain. She desired with all her soul to be a mother in Israel.

Her name was Hannah. In the New Testament, that name became *Anna*, a name that means "grace"! Let's look at how Hannah encountered a fullness of grace in her life because she so diligently sought to hear the voice of God.

Hannah had made this yearly pilgrimage to the holy place in fasting and prayer, annually pleading with God at His abode that He would hear her prayers and give her the righteous desire of her heart—children.

On this occasion, she stood near the tabernacle speaking and praying so as only God on High could hear her plight. But the high priest who *could not hear her* (and later in 1 Samuel we'll see that he also *could not hear God*) thought she was a crazy drunk:

> And it came to pass, as she continued praying before the Lord, that Eli marked her mouth.
>
> Now Hannah, she spake in her heart; only her lips moved, but her voice was not heard: therefore Eli thought she had been drunken.
>
> And Eli said unto her, How long wilt thou be drunken? put away thy wine from thee.
>
> And Hannah answered and said, No, my lord, I am a woman of a sorrowful spirit: I have drunk neither wine nor strong drink, but have poured out my soul before the Lord. (1 Samuel 1:12–15)

This is a lesson for all of us: we need to pause and ensure that we have heard and understood before we rush to judgment. This faithful, suffering woman should have been encouraged in her distress. Instead, she was misunderstood, unfairly judged, and further burdened. Worse, this heaping helping of pain was provided by one put into a position of authority to serve God's people—Eli, the high priest.

To practice what we are preaching here, we shouldn't be too quick to judge Eli. As soon as Hannah explained the reality of the circumstances, he recognized his error and blessed her: "Then Eli answered and said, Go in peace: and the God of Israel grant thee thy petition that thou hast asked of him" (1 Samuel 1:17).

What is it that Hannah most desired?

> O Lord of hosts, if thou wilt indeed look on the affliction of thine handmaid, and remember me, and not forget thine handmaid, but wilt give unto thine handmaid a man child, then I will give him unto the Lord all the days of his life, and there shall no razor come upon his head. (1 Samuel 1:11)

God heard Hannah!

After she returned from her annual visit to the temple (the ancient Israelite tabernacle), "the Lord remembered her" (1 Samuel 1:19). As her name in Hebrew reminds us (*Hannah* means "grace"), this Bible story shows us that she was blessed with His grace to receive her pleading petition.

In fact, so central to this story is God's hearing His beloved servant Hannah's prayers that Hannah named her promised son Samuel as an everlasting memorial of this most divine trait of God. The name *Samuel* in Hebrew literally means "heard of God"! Samuel is like Ishmael in the Abraham story, one who was also saved and preserved by God who hears. The Hebrew names *Samuel* and *Ishmael* both essentially come from the same Hebrew words.

Hannah's story confirms the truth, "ask and ye shall receive, knock [at the temple] and it shall be opened unto you."

CALL TO ACTION: When have you asked and received from God?

Eli Teaching the Boy Samuel ("Heard of God") to Hear the Voice of God

By Taylor Halverson

THE THEME OF HEARING IN the Hannah-Samuel story is key. The theme continues in the life of Samuel.

Soon after Samuel became a young lad, Hannah fulfilled her vow to God by dedicating Samuel's formative years to being raised by the high priest Eli at the Israelite tabernacle. Samuel was trained in the religious worship conducted there.

Like Jesus, who was also dedicated to the service of God, we hear in the Bible, "And the child Samuel grew before the Lord" (1 Samuel 1:21) and "the child Samuel grew on, and was in favour both with the Lord, and also with men" (1 Samuel 1:26).

One night after retiring for the night, Samuel had an instructive and transformative experience. In this story, notice that Eli, the high priest, could neither see, nor could he hear the voice of God. Contrast this with Samuel, who could see *and* hear. Specifically, Samuel could hear the voice of God, but he was too inexperienced to know what he was hearing.

> When Eli was laid down in his place, and his eyes began to wax dim, that *he could not see;*
> And ere the lamp of God went out in the temple of the Lord, where the ark of God was, and Samuel was laid down to sleep;
> That *the Lord called Samuel: and he answered, Here am I.*
> And he ran unto Eli, and said, Here am I; for thou calledst me. And he said, I called not; lie down again. And he went and lay down. (1 Samuel 3:2–5; emphasis added)

This scenario repeated itself with Samuel once more hearing the voice of God—mistaking it for the voice of Eli—and running to Eli, ready to be of service. Again Eli told Samuel that he had not called, and told him to return to bed. Only on the third instance did "Eli perceive that the Lord had called the child" (1 Samuel 3:8).

Eli then gave some of the most important instruction he ever delivered and that Samuel or us may ever receive in our lives: "Go, lie down: and it shall be, if [God] call thee, that thou shalt say, *Speak, Lord; for thy servant heareth*" (1 Samuel 3:9; emphasis added).

Even though Eli was blind, and was apparently deaf to hearing the voice of God, Eli could still perceive when others had heard God's voice. Perhaps one of the most important things Eli ever did in his long life of service to God was to teach Samuel how to hear, recognize, and hearken to the voice of God.

In Hebrew, Samuel's name means "heard of God," reminding us that Samuel developed the capacity to hear God, and therefore he experienced being "heard of God."

CALL TO ACTION: How are you practicing hearing the voice of God? How are you helping others to hear the voice of God? How are you helping others to recognize and act on the voice of God?

God's Still, Small Voice Reaches the Spiritually Sensitive

By Taylor Halverson

STALWART AND FAITHFUL ELIJAH FELT so dejected that He asked God to let Him die (1 Kings 19:4). He had braved the onslaught of persecution from the people, rulers, and priests of Israel and neighboring nations. He had fearlessly preached God's covenants. And like everyone else, he had physically suffered when God sent an enduring famine to the land as a consequence of the people breaking their covenant with God.

Now Elijah famished in the wilderness for lack of food and water, as had the ancient wandering Israelites. And like the ancient wandering Israelites, God did a mighty work and a wonder to feed Elijah in his distress (see 1 Kings 19:1–8). Nourished by God, Elijah roused himself to complete a spiritual and physical journey in the reverse order of the ancient Israelites. Elijah made his way from the land of Israel to Mount Sinai (also known as Mount Horeb). There, like Moses, Elijah had a transformative encounter with God.

Elijah was discouraged. He had walked hundreds of miles through blistering desert and mountains. He had fasted forty days and nights. And now at the sacred mountain of Sinai, where God had delivered the Mosaic covenant, Elijah complained to God in his searing sense of loneliness and discouragement, saying, "I have been very jealous for the LORD God of hosts: for the children of Israel have forsaken thy covenant, thrown down thine altars, and slain thy prophets with the sword; and I, *even* I only, am left; and they seek my life, to take it away" (1 Kings 19:10).

Who among us has not felt alone? Who among us has not felt criticized or misunderstood for our beliefs? Who among us has not felt that we have labored diligently and patiently in the cause of God, only to feel when we look around that we've been on a fool's errand with nothing to show for our efforts? If we can answer yes to any one of these or similar questions, we have a sense of what Elijah was feeling.

God did not reprimand Elijah. God did not punish Elijah for having natural and normal feelings, for being physically and spiritually spent. God met Elijah where he was. And from that foundation, He built Elijah further to the benefit of us all. God instructed Elijah:

> Go forth, and stand upon the mount before the LORD. And, behold, the LORD passed by, and a great and strong wind rent the mountains, and brake in pieces the rocks before

the LORD; *but* the LORD *was* not
in the wind: and after the wind an
earthquake; *but* the LORD *was* not in
the earthquake. (1 Kings 19:11)

God, who had done so many marvelous
deeds in Egypt and in Sinai, was making a
point to Elijah: "Don't seek me in grandiose or
extreme sensory experiences." No. God is far
more powerful than that. God does not need
to overpower us with His supremacy or His
majesty, even though He puts those powers
on display at times. God is in the nooks and
crannies of our life. He is with us like the wind
that caresses our face or like the warming sun
of a bright day on our eyes or like the soft
sounds of life that curl around us. "And after
the earthquake a fire; *but* the LORD *was* not in
the fire: and after the fire a still small voice" (1
Kings 19:12).

Elijah would have unmistakably seen the
effective force of the wind and felt the tremors
of the earthquake and seen the blazing light
of burning fire. Any one of these could have
firmly demonstrated God's power to Elijah.
But God was not trying to overpower Elijah's
physical senses. God wanted to tune Elijah's
spiritual senses, especially to the quiet, nearly
imperceptible sound of God's voice that is
always there if we would focus and listen!

God's voice is like the air we breathe. Always
there. Always sustaining us. Almost never

noticed until we need it most or when it is seemingly not immediately available.

Of all the characteristics of God that are paradoxically easy to overlook, His still, small voice is the most enduring, sustaining, and accessible.

CALL TO ACTION: What devices or experiences or thoughts can you turn off and tune out so that you can tune in to the voice of God? What actions do you need to start doing to find this peace? What actions do you need to stop doing to experience God's voice more fully in your life?

Strong Characteristics of the Voice of God: Psalms

By Taylor Halverson

THE STORY OF ELIJAH TEACHES us of the power inherent in God's still, small voice. We learn from Elijah that we need not seek after eye-popping experiences with God to know of His love and care.

Nevertheless, God is still the Creator and power of the universe. Other scriptures speak of His all-encompassing majesty, His unsearchable strength, and His unfathomable ways. Ancient Israelite poets described enduring characteristics of God focusing on His voice. In Psalm 29, look at all the adjectives used to describe the nature of God's voice:

> The voice of the Lord is upon the waters: the God of glory thundereth: the Lord is upon many waters.
>
> The voice of the Lord is powerful; the voice of the Lord is full of majesty.
>
> The voice of the Lord breaketh the cedars; yea, the Lord breaketh the cedars of Lebanon. . . .

The voice of the Lord divideth the flames of fire.

The voice of the Lord shaketh the wilderness; the Lord shaketh the wilderness of Kadesh.

The voice of the Lord maketh the hinds to calve, and discovereth the forests: and in his temple doth every one speak of his glory.

The Lord sitteth upon the flood; yea, the Lord sitteth King for ever.

The Lord will give strength unto his people; the Lord will bless his people with peace. (Psalms 29:3–5, 7–11)

CALL TO ACTION: After reading this psalm, what new knowledge about the voice of God and His nature and attributes have you gained? How have your trust and confidence in the voice God increased?

Wisdom Comes from Hearing the Voice of God: Proverbs

By Taylor Halverson

THE BOOK OF PROVERBS IN the Bible was written and preserved to teach people true wisdom. Its opening passages declare this very purpose:

> [Read this book] to know wisdom and instruction; to perceive the words of understanding;
> To receive the instruction of wisdom, justice, and judgment, and equity. (Proverbs 1:2–3)

Later in this opening chapter, the inspired author of Proverbs speaks to readers as if they are beloved sons or daughters. Listen to the beautiful role parents play in helping their children learn to hear the voice of God and thereby achieve wisdom:

> The fear [or humble acknowledgment] of the Lord is the beginning of knowledge: but fools despise wisdom and instruction.

> My [child], hear the instruction
> of thy father, and forsake not the
> law of thy mother. (Proverbs 1:7–
> 8)

Wise children hear the righteous counsel of their father and mother. They gain more wisdom and enter into the path of the knowledge of God.

Proverbs continues this theme of gaining wisdom by hearing God. Proverbs depicts wisdom as a woman navigating the ancient city streets, purposely calling out to any who would listen to heed her voice of wisdom and warming:

> Wisdom   crieth   without;   she
> uttereth her voice in the streets:
> She crieth in the chief place of
> concourse, in the openings of the
> gates: in the city she uttereth her
> words, saying,
> How long, ye simple ones, will
> ye love simplicity? and the scorners
> delight in their scorning, and fools
> hate knowledge? (Proverbs 1:20–22)

Sadly, some are too distracted by the things of this world, or are too ashamed of the things of God, to hear and heed the voice of God's wisdom wandering throughout their lives: "For the turning away of the simple shall slay them, and the prosperity of fools shall destroy them" (Proverbs 1:32). But the promise endures for those who hearken to the wise woman representing God's knowledge: "But whoso hearkeneth unto me shall dwell safely, and shall be quiet from fear of evil" (Proverbs 1:33).

CALL TO ACTION: How has knowing God led to wisdom in your life? How has respecting and loving God led to knowledge and safety?

The Voice of God Calls Us to Receive His Purging Love

By Taylor Halverson

TODAY AS WELL AS IN the past, God calls prophets to teach us to know His voice. One of the greatest prophets of all time to hear and hearken to the God's call was Isaiah. He records for us His beautiful prophetic appointment in Isaiah 6.

Isaiah had a vision of God at the temple. Accompanying God were members of His heavenly host, including beings that were bright light fire called Seraphim (the word *seraphim* in Hebrew means "bright, burning ones"). Faithful, humble Isaiah realized his low and fallen state among God and these pure heavenly beings. He exclaimed in anguish, "Woe is me! for I am undone; because I am a man of unclean lips, and I dwell in the midst of a people of unclean lips: for mine eyes have seen the King, the Lord of hosts" (Isaiah 6:5).

The unexpected but necessary then took place. One of the heavenly beings took a flaming coal from the temple altar and placed it upon Isaiah's lips to demonstrate symbolic purging, saying, "This hath touched thy lips;

and thine iniquity is taken away, and thy sin purged" (Isaiah 6:7). We are promised the same baptism of fire when we repent and enter into a covenant relationship with God.

What happens after we have felt the refiner's fire by willingly entering into a covenant with God? We, like Isaiah, will be able to hear and positively respond to the voice of God inviting us to join Him in His work: "I heard the voice of the Lord, saying, Whom shall I send, and who will go for us? Then said I, Here am I; send me" (Isaiah 6:8).

CALL TO ACTION: When have you felt the refiner's fire purging and healing you? What did you desire to do after you felt the surging love of God in your life?

Promising to Hear and Obey God No Matter the Circumstances

By Taylor Halverson

JEREMIAH LIVED AT A TIME of extreme turmoil, living in Jerusalem during the same time period as Lehi. The hard-heartedness of the Israelites was so pervasive that Lehi had to flee for his life with his family from Jerusalem.

During these years, the Babylonians threatened the peace and security of the people in Israel. Some living in Jerusalem taught that since the temple was in their midst and because they had a Davidic king on the throne, they would be safe—that God would protect them from the Babylonians no matter what. Jeremiah and Lehi taught otherwise. They taught with words of soberness that only repentance and covenanting with God would protect the people from the Babylonians. For these teachings, Jeremiah was thrown into a dungeon prison and Lehi was run out of town.

Jeremiah was later released from prison. But the situation did not improve. So intense was the conflict in Jerusalem over how to respond to the Babylonian threat that a small-scale civil war broke out among those living in Jerusalem. People feared for their lives because they did not know if one of the contending factions would slay them.

In those very difficult circumstances, some of the people came to realize that their only security was in trusting in and hearkening to God. Coming to Jeremiah, they petitioned his help and the help of God. Jeremiah promised to seek the Lord's will. And the people put themselves under covenant to obey God no matter what:

> Then they said to Jeremiah, The Lord be a true and faithful witness between us, if we do not even according to all things for the which the Lord thy God shall send thee to us.
>
> Whether it be good, or whether it be [unexpected], *we will obey the voice of the Lord our God*, to whom we send thee; *that it may be well with us, when we obey the voice of the Lord our God*. (Jeremiah 42:5–6; emphasis added)

Like the poor among the Zoramites, some of the citizens of ancient Jerusalem had been compelled to humility because of their circumstances. They were willing to covenant to hear and obey God in all things. As Alma taught the Zoramites (see Alma 32:13–16), how blessed are we if we are compelled to be humble. And how much more blessed are we if we *choose* to be humble. That humility is demonstrated by a frank and sincere willingness to hear and obey God in all things.

CALL TO ACTION: Make and keep covenants with God to obey Him in all things. That is a powerful way to hear the voice of God in your life.

God Hears Our Voice in Our Distress

By Taylor Halverson

THE FIVE CHAPTERS OF THE book of Lamentations are heart-rending sobs of pain and sorrow. This book is traditionally attributed to the prophet Jeremiah, who documented the soul-crushing suffering inflicted upon Jerusalem and her inhabitants at the hands of the conquering Babylonians. Jeremiah acknowledges that God is in charge and that His ways are just. Still, Jeremiah's prayers reach to the heavens, seeking the favor of God that He would deliver those who recognize His Kingship.

In our lives, we all suffer. We experience some suffering because of our choices. Some suffering is a consequence of other people's choices. Some suffering follows from natural causes over which we may have little to no control.

Regardless of the source of our suffering, we do have a choice.

We can choose to repent of the things we've done that have caused pain to ourselves or others. And we can choose to forgive when we experience pain caused by others (though that does not mean we need to stay in painful or destructive circumstances).

In all these things, God is constantly there. He hears us! Yes, this book is primarily about hearing the voice of God in our lives. Paradoxically, though, sometimes we experience and hear the voice of God when *He* hears *us*, especially when we are distressed.

These are the words of Jeremiah on that very theme. He was so thoroughly enmeshed in suffering and difficulty that his words seem to drown before he uttered them:

> Mine enemies chased me sore, like a bird, without cause.
> They have cut off my life in the dungeon, and cast a stone upon me.
> Waters flowed over mine head; *then* I said, I am cut off.
> (Lamentations 3:52–54)

In his greatest moment of distress, at the very precipice of despair, Jeremiah experienced the saving power that comes from God hearing His children. Then following the lead of God who hears, Jeremiah heard God whispering those most soothing words, "fear not":

> I called upon thy name, O LORD, out of the low dungeon.
> *Thou hast heard my voice*: hide not thine ear at my breathing, at my cry.

Thou drewest near in the day *that* I called upon thee: *thou saidst, Fear not.*

O Lord, thou hast pleaded the causes of my soul; thou hast redeemed my life. (Lamentations 3:55–58; emphasis added)

CALL TO ACTION: Remember that God loves you. He knows you. He knows that you suffer and struggle. And He will hear you as you listen to His voice.

Those Who Hear the Voice of God Build His Temples and Serve There

By Taylor Halverson

LATER IN THE OLD TESTAMENT we find Zechariah, a significant prophet whose words are too often overlooked. I love the Hebrew meaning of his name because it witnesses of a key characteristic and strength of God: "Jehovah is righteous."

Zechariah lived to see the Jews return from Babylonian exile and to begin rebuilding Jerusalem (about 520 BC). The leaders of Israel returned with high hopes of restoration, believing that God would be with them and that this time the Israelites would fully turn to God—unlike many of their ancestors, who had fallen into strange paths or who had been distracted by the things of this world.

But the times of Zechariah were not much different than the generations of Israelites before his time. Zechariah had to witness, urge, preach, warn, and invite the people to turn to God. The primary challenge Zechariah faced is that the people slacked in their efforts to rebuild the walls of Jerusalem and the temple. They were discouraged. The land had been ruined, and an incredible amount of effort was required to return the land, the city, and the temple to their former glory.

Seeking to rouse the people to physical and spiritual energetic commitment to the cause of God, Zechariah declared a series of dreams or visions he had about God's purposes for Jerusalem and the temple. Zechariah learned that God wanted His temple rebuilt. He shared these words with the people:

> And they that are far off shall come and build in the temple of the LORD, and ye shall know that the LORD of hosts hath sent me unto you. And this shall come to pass, if ye will diligently obey the voice of the LORD your God. (Zechariah 6:15)

Zechariah paired a challenge and a promise. If the people obeyed the voice of God, He would bring additional help and resources to build the temple.

So it is in our day. We live in a time of unprecedented temple building throughout the world. God is raising up people and resources to build His kingdom, symbolized by temples. As we hearken to His voice, we will see an acceleration of the rolling forth of the kingdom of God.

We demonstrate that we have heard God by building temples and by doing the sacred work of salvation that takes place within the walls of those hallowed buildings.

CALL TO ACTION: Visit the temple, contribute to the construction of a temple, or participate in ancestral work. Each of these actions is a form of hearing the voice of God.

What the Marys Heard

By Lisa Halverson

AT THE BEGINNING AND THE end of His mortal life as well as in the midst of His mortal ministry, Jesus was blessed by the faith of three women, all named Mary. These Marys listened to the voice of the Lord and His messengers. Let's examine their unparalleled moments, when listening was crucial to their incredible experiences.

One moment, the Annunciation, marked Christ's conception. The second, a simple moment of teaching among friends, was unremarkable but for the crucial truth it taught about priorities to those who would listen. The final, at a tomb in a garden just outside Jerusalem, marked the revelation to all humankind of His Resurrection. The next three chapters will explore how each of these Marys experienced hearing God.

Mary, the Mother of Jesus Christ

By Lisa Halverson

AS A YOUNG WOMAN—not much more than a girl—Mary, daughter of Anna and Joachim, heard and saw the angel Gabriel. He spoke these words to her: "Hail, thou that art highly favoured, the Lord is with thee; blessed art thou among women" (Luke 1:28).

Mary "was troubled at his saying, and cast in her mind what manner of salutation this should be" (Luke 1:29). Her confusion is understandable. Though of the line of David, her family held no great position or wealth. They lived in Nazareth, the backwaters of the Roman Empire, in a village of two hundred to four hundred people, where everyone knew everyone else. By order of the Jewish queen Salome Alexandra one hundred years before, the boys were literate. But their families were farmers and stonecutters (translated as "carpenters" in the King James Version of the Bible), finding work an hour's walk away in Sepphoris, the opulent Greek-style regional capital being built by Herod Antipas. In her circumstance, Mary may not have felt particularly favored or blessed. In any case, it was clearly an unusual "manner of salutation," and she was confused and even a bit afraid.

Seeing Mary's confusion, Gabriel added: "Fear not, Mary, for thou hast found favour with God. And, behold, thou shalt conceive in thy womb, and bring forth a son, and shalt call his name JESUS" (Luke 1:30–31).

Still confused and expressing "How shall this be, seeing I know not a man?," Mary continued to listen and was told that "with God nothing shall be impossible" (Luke 1:37). Her ready response to hearing Gabriel's incredible message was faithful and trusting: "Behold the handmaid of the Lord; be it unto me according to thy word" (Luke 1:38).

Many have wondered how she, not much older than a child, could have such faith. It may have come from her close listening to Gabriel's words. Remember what he said:

> Hail, thou that art *highly favoured, the Lord is with thee. . . .*
> *Fear not*, Mary: for *thou hast found favour with God.* (Luke 1:28, 30; emphasis added)

First, her fears were assuaged as she heard that the Lord was with her. And if He was with her, she could not fail! Additionally, the assurance that she was "highly favoured" had meanings beyond simply being a favorite. It also meant to be graced and honored with blessings and to be made acceptable. Before Gabriel delivered the most earth-shattering news she would ever hear, he told her that God would make her acceptable. Hearing these words, she knew that the Lord would indeed magnify her for this sacred and holy calling. He loved her, and through His grace, she was enough.

By the time Mary saw her cousin Elisabeth, she had let the words she heard sink deep down into her very being: "My soul doth magnify the Lord," she exclaimed upon seeing Elisabeth! (Luke 1:46).

In the passage that follows (often called the *Magnificat*), Mary testifies of the same grace she heard from Gabriel:

> [H]e that is mighty hath done to me great things; and holy is his name.
>
> And his mercy is on them that fear him from generation to generation.
>
> He hath shewed strength with his arm; he hath scattered the proud in the imagination of their hearts.
>
> He hath put down the mighty from their seats, and exalted them of low degree.
>
> He hath filled the hungry with good things; and the rich he hath sent empty away.
>
> He hath holpen his servant Israel, in remembrance of his mercy. (Luke 1:49–52)

This beautiful testimony grew deep during the three-month period that would have included morning sickness; derision, shame, and exclusion from many of her small-town neighbors; and nearly the end of her betrothal to her beloved Joseph. Surely she was a woman of immeasurable faith. Still, how was she so certain of God's goodness when her own life was so tumultuous? Because she had listened closely when a messenger from God spoke to her, telling her that there was no need to fear because God was with her and would "favour" her—as He favors all of His children who come unto Him!—by magnifying her and making her equal to the assignments that lay before her.

CALL TO ACTION: This story is the message God gives to each of us. Have we heard Him?

Mary, the Friend of Christ and Sister of Martha and Lazarus

By Lisa Halverson

MARY, MARTHA, AND LAZARUS WERE among Christ's closest friends during His adult life and ministry. He often stayed at their home (see Matthew 21:17) in Bethany (literally, *house of the poor*), a village located on the southeastern slope of the Mount of Olives and a mere two miles from Jerusalem. Christ's empathy for the sisters and love for their brother was clear when He wept with Mary and Martha outside Lazarus's tomb (see John 11:35), even though He knew He would raise Lazarus from the dead in only a few short minutes.

We are all familiar with the story of Mary and Martha in Luke 10. As Martha bustled about with preparations for the Lord, Mary "sat at Jesus' feet, and heard his word" (Luke 10:39). I don't want to criticize Martha for serving as she was taught a woman of her day should serve: Cleaning the house, preparing the food, hushing the children. With my hearing loss, when we have guests and the house fills with the noise of many people, I sometimes bypass the conversations I will struggle to hear and instead immerse myself in preparing, tidying, and otherwise being "careful and troubled about many things" (Luke 10:41).

But Mary's actions remind me of the times when I recognize that I *need* to hear. I too sit close. Once, at the end of a retreat with about forty teaching colleagues and students, we spent the last evening gathered in a large circle, lights out except for a small candle, sharing our most important learnings from our time together. With my poor hearing, there was no way I was going to pick up what was said in hushed voices across the dark room. I chose to sit on the floor in front of each person, pushing myself a few feet every time the candle was passed to the next speaker. When I think back on that night, I could wonder if any students laughed to see a teacher inching along the dirty log-house floor. Instead, I hope they left knowing I cared for them and valued what they had to say; sitting at their feet was my way of ensuring that I heard their every word.

We don't know what exact topic Jesus spoke on that night. But Mary realized that she *needed* to hear His every word. She too knew that "one thing is needful," and she chose "that good part" (Luke 10:42). In a small village named for the poor who could not reside in the nearby, majestic Jerusalem, Mary's floor may not have been perfectly clean either. (Perhaps that is what Martha bustled about to clean!)

Women often did not sit close to a man not of their family, but Mary focused on that good and needful part and sat, listening to the Lord.

Whatever she heard, it surely fed her testimony at the time of her brother's death: "Lord, if thou hadst been here, my brother had not died" (John 11:32).

And it surely prepared her for what had never before occurred, when the Savior "cried with a loud voice, Lazarus, come forth" (John 11:43). Like his sister, Lazarus heard his Master. "He that was dead came forth" (John 11: 44).

This is another message God gives to us—that His voice is the one we must heed. Listening to His word is "good" and "needful." But even more, it is life-giving, full of power even to overcome death.

CALL TO ACTION: Will we sit at His feet and hear Him?

Mary Magdalene, the First Witness of the Resurrected Lord

By Lisa Halverson

WHEN SHE IS FIRST INTRODUCED in the Gospel of Luke, we learn that Mary called Magdalene had seven devils cast out of her (see Luke 8:2; the same chapter also tells of Christ's calming of the tempest, healing of the woman with an issue of blood, and raising of Jairus's daughter from the dead). We do not know exactly what it meant to be rid of devils, but at the time mental health disorders—including debilitating depression, disabling anxiety, eating disorders, and addictive behaviors—were all often attributed to devils. Why was it said Mary had seven devils? Is seven used symbolically, to mean that they were completely, overwhelmingly present in Mary's psyche? Is it that she seemed plagued by more than one simple disorder?

Whatever her ailment, after being healed of the Lord Mary became one of His most (perhaps even the most) devoted of His followers. She was present at the cross (see Matthew 27:56), despite the inevitable harassment a subjugated Jewish woman would have faced from the jeering Roman guards. She participated in the burial preparation of the Lord's broken and bleeding body (see Mark 15:47), even though this would render her ritually unclean and unable to participate in holy rituals for seven days thereafter. And days later, she was weeping at His tomb on the morning that He rose (see John 20:11), even though no one seemed to understand that that was His next step.

The story that follows teaches us about listening to the Lord. We know that "as she wept, [Mary] stooped down, and looked into the sepulcher, and seeth two angels in white" (John 20:11–12), who asked her why she wept. She heard and understood the angels, but she did not understand the magnitude of their presence and what was to follow. She answered, "Because they have taken away my Lord, and I know not where they have laid him" (John 20:13).

At that point she turned about and "saw Jesus standing, and knew not that it was Jesus." He even spoke to her, asking, "Woman, why weepest thou? whom sleekest thou?" (John 20:15). At this point she both heard and saw the resurrected Christ, but still did not recognize Him. Even as she answered Him, it appears from the text that she turned away from Him again, supposing Him to be a mere gardener.

It wasn't a change in the Lord's appearance that "opens her eyes." Rather, it was Christ calling unto her by her own, individual name: "Jesus saith unto her, Mary. She turned herself, and saith unto him, Rabboni; which is to say, Master" (John 20:16). When Mary heard the sound of her own name, both her eyes and her ears were opened to recognize the Risen Lord.

Of course, it is human nature to pay better attention better when we know something—or someone—affects us personally. But perhaps it is something deeper too. Just as I stated earlier that we will recognize the Lord because we have practiced listening to His voice and, in so doing, have become like Him, so too the Lord recognizes us because He has been there, listening to us (hopefully because we have used our voices to cry out to him—though I suspect He is a pretty good speechreader as well!). He knows us by name and reaches out to us individually. If we are listening to His individual gestures, we too can recognize Him. In some of my most beautiful blessings—including, but not limited to, my patriarchal blessing—I have heard the Lord's voice, spoken through His representatives, reminding me that He knows me by name and He knows the innermost workings of my heart.

At this most remarkable of *all* moments in the world's history, Mary heard her name and recognized the Savior of the world, suddenly no simple gardener to her eyes but the resplendent and risen Lord of all.

CALL TO ACTION: Can we also listen as He speaks to us, individually and intimately, eager to show forth miracles in our lives too?

Seek to Hear the Voice of
the Shepherd

By Taylor Halverson

ONE OF THE BEST SCRIPTURES in the New Testament to teach us about how to hear the voice of God is found in John 10. Significantly, the chapter right before, John 9, is devoted to the power of seeing and acting on truth, especially of seeing God and following Him, while John 10 is focused on learning to hear God.

Remember that in John 9, Jesus healed a blind man on the Sabbath in the temple. The Jewish authorities were apoplectic with rage that their traditions of "no Sabbath work" was so brazenly violated in the most sacred location. With persecuting questions, the authorities badgered the blind man. At the culmination of John 9, the blind man (who now could see) queried incredulously of the supposedly all-seeing and wise religious leaders when they asked him yet again how he was healed: "I have told you already, and ye did not hear: wherefore would ye hear *it* again? will ye also be his disciples?" (John 9:27). This passage in John 9 transitions us from the theme of being healed of our blindness by God so that we can see Him to the theme of hearing God.

The religious leaders at the time of Jesus could neither see nor hear the truth of God.

In John 10, Jesus turned to the theme of hearing. He used the metaphor of a shepherd to symbolize Himself, and He symbolized His people as sheep. Listen to what He taught about how to hear the voice of the Good Shepherd.

> *The sheep hear his voice*: and he calleth his own sheep by name, and leadeth them out.
>
> And when he putteth forth his own sheep, he goeth before them, and the sheep follow him: for *they know his voice*.
>
> And a stranger will they not follow, but will flee from him: for *they know not the voice of strangers*. (John 10:3–5; emphasis added)

When the Jews heard these words from Jesus, they were angry. Thinking He was mad or that He was the devil, they challenged Jesus to declare His identity. In utter solemnity and peace, He spoke these words of truth:

> I told you [who I am], and ye believed not: the works that I do in my Father's name, they bear witness of me.

But ye believe not, because ye are not of my sheep, as I said unto you.

My sheep hear my voice, and I know them, and they follow me:

And I give unto them eternal life; and they shall never perish, neither shall any *man* pluck them out of my hand. (John 10:25–28; emphasis added)

Though we all stumble and fall in our attempts to hear and follow the Good Shepherd, know that He is ever with us. Like sheep who seek to be near their shepherd and seek to heed his voice, we too will be brought into our Shepherd's fold and will be protected by His mighty grace.

We do not have to strive to save ourselves. He has already accomplished that work, which is why we call Him the Savior. We need only to stay close to Him by hearing His voice.

CALL TO ACTION: How much time do you spend tuning your heart to the voice of God compared to how much time you spend tuning in to hear the cacophonous voices of the world?

Hearing God Leads to Salvation:
The Foundation of the
Book of Mormon

By Taylor Halverson

HEARING THE VOICE OF GOD serves as a consistent theme throughout the Book of Mormon. By our count, there are more than 280 instances of *hear*, *heard*, *hearing*, *hearken*, and other words with *hear* at their roots in the Book of Mormon. This count does not include words like *listen*, *call*, *calling*, *talk*, *voice*, or many other words that represent speaking and hearing.

There are many hundreds of instances of listening, being called, hearing, speaking, and hearkening throughout the Book of Mormon. This constant thematic refrain is meant to remind us that our spiritual salvation depends on tuning our spiritual ears to capturing the ever-flowing cascade of truth available to God's children.

1 Nephi 1 begins with an action-packed introduction that grabs us by the collar and won't let us go. Only six verses into one of the most important books ever composed, we are thrust into the retelling of Lehi's awe-inspiring

theophany. Nephi tells us that Lehi "heard much" (1 Nephi 1:6). But what led to Lehi receiving this grand vision of God and His plan? Nephi tells us, "Wherefore it came to pass that my father, Lehi, as he went forth prayed unto the Lord, yea, even with all his heart, in behalf of his people" (1 Nephi 1:5).

At the cost of potentially losing his life, Lehi then went forth to teach the people of Jerusalem what he had seen and *heard*. In contrast to soft-hearted Lehi who had spiritual ears ready to hear, the people of Jerusalem turned to murderous anger "when [they] heard these things [and] they were angry with him; yea, even as with the prophets of old, whom they had cast out, and stoned, and slain; and they also sought his life, that they might take it away" (1 Nephi 1:20). Nephi concludes this portion of his narrative, where the life of his father stands on the brink, with one of the most beautiful witnesses of God's nature found anywhere in scripture—what we and others call Nephi's thesis:

> But behold, I, Nephi, will show unto you that the tender mercies of the Lord are over all those whom he hath chosen, because of their faith, to make them mighty even unto the power of deliverance. (1 Nephi 1:20)

This one statement from Nephi appears to serve as an orienting theme for the rest of his writings.

The lesson for us that we see in the opening pages of the Book of Mormon is that we too should go forth and pray unto the Lord with all our hearts, especially on behalf of others.

CALL TO ACTION: Make a plan to include others and their needs in your prayers and petitions to God. What do you learn from this service?

Hearing the Word of God Can Lead to an Outpouring of Revelatory Truth

By Taylor Halverson

WHILE IN THE WILDERNESS WITH his family, Lehi experienced a profound dream of the tree of life. Moved by hearing his father's description of the dream and the plan of salvation and love of God represented in that dream, Nephi wanted know for himself. Nephi recounted:

> And it came to pass after I, Nephi, having *heard all the words of my father*, concerning the things which he saw in a vision, and also the things which he spake by the power of the Holy Ghost, which power he received by faith on the Son of God—and the Son of God was the Messiah who should come—*I, Nephi, was desirous also that I might see, and hear, and know of these things*, by the power of the Holy Ghost, which is the gift of God unto all those who diligently seek him, as well in times

of old as in the time that he should
manifest himself unto the children of
men. (1 Nephi 10:17; emphasis added)

Soon after Nephi's righteous desire
swelled within his soul, he was transported to
a high mountain and there received his own
individualized experience with the tree of life as
well as many other truths (see 1 Nephi 11–14).

The lesson to be learned here is that we
should let the words of truth we hear from
others stir our souls to likewise want to see and
hear and know as they have. We are told that
each of us will receive a gift of the Spirit. Some
will have the gift of faith. Some will have the
gift of revelation. Others will have the gift of
believing those who have the gift of revelation.
We can acquire and develop all good gifts from
God, and Nephi is an absolute example. He had
the gift to believe the words of those who had
the gift of revelation. And by acting on that
initial gift of believing others, he grew into
the gift of revelation. In other words, he heard
those who had heard the word of God, and he
then learned how to hear as other had heard.

All of us need teachers, instructors, friends,
family, and mentors who can show us how to
better hear the voice of God in our lives. As
we watch and learn from them, and then as
we deliberately practice more faithfulness, we
too will gain greater gifts of enlarged spiritual
capacity. But learning does not stop. As we

develop our hearing sensitivities, we should be mindful to teach and mentor those who could learn from us.

CALL TO ACTION: When was the last time you heard the voice of God? Did that voice come directly to you? Or was it through an inspired leader, friend, or family member? Or in some other divine way?

Hearkening to God Is Holding to the Iron Rod

By Taylor Halverson

AFTER NEPHI'S EXPANSIVE REVELATORY EXPE-
RIENCE and hearing and seeing much from God,
he sadly found his brothers having a contentious
argument about Lehi's dream. Wearied by such
faithlessness, Nephi queried them if they had
asked knowledge from God in order to resolve the
issue by saying, "Have ye inquired of the Lord?" (1
Nephi 15:8).

Nephi's brothers' response is telling and
indicative of those who miss out on knowing
God more fully because they do not believe that
God would want to disclose more of Himself to
them: "And they said unto me: We have not; for
the Lord maketh no such thing known unto us"
(1 Nephi 15:9).

Nephi's brothers did not realize that it was
their false belief that created a self-fulfilling
prophecy "proving" their fake claim that God
did not want to speak to them. Nephi corrected
this falsehood with a principle any of us can
apply today for positive effect:

> Do ye not remember the things which the Lord hath said?—If ye will not harden your hearts, and ask me in faith, believing that ye shall receive, with diligence in keeping my commandments, surely these things shall be made known unto you. (1 Nephi 15:11)

When we wonder how we can better know God, feel His presence, and hear His loving voice in our lives, we might ask ourselves these questions: Do we believe that God is there? Do we believe that He loves us? Have we already sought for and recognized God's hand in our lives? God stands ever ready to fill our lives with love, power, purpose, and meaning. We must be willing to receive. Seeking for and listening to His voice is a key ingredient in our spiritual development.

Nephi's words did have an effect on his brothers, and soon they were asking him questions and listening to his responses. One of the great truths revealed in this exchange started with this question: "What meaneth the rod which our father saw, that led to the tree?" (1 Nephi 15:23).

Nephi explained that those who hear the voice of God are those who hold tight to the rod of iron. In other words, as we hear and enact the words of God, we are symbolically holding to the safety of the rod of iron that leads us to Jesus, represented by the tree of life.

And I said unto them that it was the word of God; and *whoso would hearken unto the word of God*, and would hold fast unto it, they *would never perish*; neither could the temptations and the fiery darts of the adversary overpower them unto blindness, to lead them away to destruction.

Wherefore, I, Nephi, did exhort them to give heed unto the word of the Lord; yea, I did exhort them with all the energies of my soul, and with all the faculty which I possessed, that they would give heed to the word of God and remember to keep his commandments always in all things. (1 Nephi 15:24–25; emphasis added)

Hearkening to the word of God means that we have our souls ready to be planted with the seeds of His word so that these might sprout into trees of eternal life. Hearkening to the word of God means that we seek to hear God; to recognize His voice; and to record, preserve, and organize His word. We must reflect upon His word. We must act upon His word. And we should share these words with those around us.

CALL TO ACTION: Document in a personal journal one way in which you have hearkened to the word of God and describe the result.

Hearing Isaiah in the Book of Mormon

By Taylor Halverson

WHEN NEPHI AND JACOB QUOTED Isaiah at length, they used the following pattern: One chapter explained the purpose for quoting Isaiah, another chapter or more quoted Isaiah, and then one or more chapters explained further why they quoted Isaiah. We see this pattern in 1 Nephi 19–22. In 1 Nephi 19, Nephi explains why he will quote Isaiah. He quotes Isaiah in 1 Nephi 20–21. And then in 1 Nephi 22, Nephi explains why he is quoting Isaiah.

The first time Nephi quotes Isaiah at length in the Book of Mormon, he introduces the venerable prophet through the theme of hearing:

> Wherefore I spake unto them, saying: *Hear ye the words of the prophet [Isaiah]*, ye who are a remnant of the house of Israel, a branch who have been broken off; *hear ye the words of the prophet*, which were written unto all the house of Israel, and liken them unto yourselves, *that ye may have hope*

as well as your brethren from whom ye have been broken off; for after this manner has the prophet written. (1 Nephi 19:24; emphasis added)

Why did Nephi quote Isaiah? Why did Nephi implore us to hear Isaiah? That we might have hope!

Not only did Nephi focus on the theme of hearing when introducing the words of Isaiah to his readers, the initial words of Isaiah that Nephi quoted also center on the role of hearing:

Hearken and hear this, O house of Jacob, who are called by the name of Israel, and are come forth out of the waters of Judah, or out of the waters of baptism, who swear by the name of the Lord, and make mention of the God of Israel, yet they swear not in truth nor in righteousness. (1 Nephi 20:1; emphasis added. See also Isaiah 48:1)

God's prophets plead with us to see signposts that show us the way to safety if we will only open our eyes. Hearing the word of God is like recognizing those signposts that show us the way to safety.

Nephi loved the prophets of old because they spoke so clearly of the covenant path and God's everlasting nature and character. In what can be described as "by the mouth of two or more witnesses," Nephi followed the lead of Isaiah, who urged us to hear God.

CALL TO ACTION: How have you heard truth from God confirmed by multiple witnesses?

Staying on the Covenant Path Requires Hearing God's Servants

By Taylor Halverson

GOD PROMISED ABRAHAM AND HIS posterity the possibility of enduring prosperity to become a blessing to the entire world (see Genesis 12:1–3). Those divine promises were renewed for the house of Israel through Moses at Mount Sinai. There God revealed the Ten Commandments as covenantal instructions for how His people were to show covenantal love and loyalty to Him as their God and King. God raises up prophets in each dispensation to teach us our covenantal duties, with Moses being the example for later generations of the type of prophet from whom they should anticipate hearing.

Nephi taught his people within this context—that prophets like Moses, called of God, would teach the people their covenantal obligations. Nephi underscored that *hearing the prophet like Moses* was foundational to receiving the fullness of God's promises:

> And the Lord will surely prepare a
> way for his people, unto the fulfilling

of the words of Moses, which he spake, saying: A prophet shall the Lord your God raise up unto you, like unto me; *him shall ye hear in all things whatsoever he shall say unto you.* And it shall come to pass that all *those who will not hear that prophet shall be cut off* from among the people. (1 Nephi 22:20; emphasis added)

Though there have been and will be many prophets like Moses, who faithfully reveal God's will so that His people will stay firm on the covenant path, Jesus Christ is the fullest fulfilment of Nephi's prophecy: "And now I, Nephi, declare unto you, that this prophet of whom Moses spake was the Holy One of Israel; wherefore, he shall execute judgment in righteousness" (1 Nephi 22:21).

CALL TO ACTION: What has God directed His leaders to teach that you should implement in your life today? Find a teaching from Jesus and strive to live it for a week.

Listening to Wise Elders

By Taylor Halverson

BEFORE PASSING FROM THIS EARTH, Lehi gathered his family to give them final counsel and blessings. There are other instances of such final testimonies or farewell addresses elsewhere in scripture, such as when the patriarch Jacob gave patriarchal blessings to each of his sons (see Genesis 49), when the prophet Samuel left his final testimony with the Israelites before he died (see 1 Samuel 12), and when King Benjamin delivered his final and masterful speech to his people (see Mosiah 2–6). These speeches are significant, for they contain a summary of the most important doctrines and teachings that a leader wishes his people to hear and do.

Lehi reminded his family and his people to *hear*. Spiritual safety, he told them, was found only in hearing and acting on the truth. Let's listen again to what Lehi told his people. To Laman and Lemuel specifically, he said,

> Awake! and arise from the dust, and *hear the words of a trembling parent*, whose limbs ye must soon lay down in the cold and silent grave, from whence no traveler can return; a few

more days and I go the way of all the earth. (2 Nephi 1:14; emphasis added)

Lehi later pronounced a promise upon all his sons that echoed throughout the ages of Nephite history. The promise swung on the hinge of *hearing*:

> And now my son, Laman, and also Lemuel and Sam, and also my sons who are the sons of Ishmael, behold, *if ye will hearken unto the voice of Nephi ye shall not perish.* And if ye will hearken unto him I leave unto you a blessing, yea, even my first blessing. But *if ye will not hearken unto him I take away my first blessing,* yea, even my blessing, and it shall rest upon him. (2 Nephi 1:28–29; emphasis added)

Who has given you loving and righteous counsel before they departed this life? Who in your life is like Lehi, Samuel, patriarch Jacob, or King Benjamin? What have you learned from them? How have you grown closer to the Lord? How have your abilities to hear God in your life increased because of the testimony of an older family member or friend?

CALL TO ACTION: Take a moment to receive counsel and advice from a wise elder or trusted friend.

We Will Hear the Words of God in the Latter Days by Means of the Book of Mormon

By Taylor Halverson

ISAIAH PROPHESIED OF THE COMING forth of the Book of Mormon. As an inspired poet and prophet, Isaiah used vivid imagery to teach that this latter-day marvelous work and a wonder, the Book of Mormon, would sweep the earth with truth:

> And the vision of all is become unto you as the words of a book that is sealed, which men deliver to one that is learned, saying, Read this, I pray thee: and he saith, I cannot; for it is sealed. . . .
> *And in that day shall the deaf hear the words of the book*, and the eyes of the blind shall see out of obscurity, and out of darkness.
> The meek also shall increase their joy in the Lord, and the poor among men shall *rejoice in the Holy One of Israel.* (Isaiah 29:11, 18–19; emphasis added)

It is not the learned or the proud or the self-important who will know and understand the words of the sealed book (the Book of Mormon). Rather, it will be those who trust God, those He makes to hear because of their meekness and humility.

Nephi later expanded upon Isaiah's prophetic words that describe the Book of Mormon rising out of the dust as if in a whisper. We are to listen carefully to its message:

> But behold, the righteous that *hearken unto the words of the prophets*, and destroy them not, *but look forward unto Christ* with steadfastness for the signs which are given, notwithstanding all persecution – behold, *they are they which shall not perish.* . . .
>
> . . . the words of the righteous shall be written, and *the prayers of the faithful shall be heard*, and all those who have dwindled in unbelief shall not be forgotten.
>
> For those who shall be destroyed shall speak unto them out of the ground, and their speech shall be low out of the dust, and their voice shall be as one that hath a familiar spirit; for the Lord God will give unto him power, that he may whisper concerning them, even as it were out of the ground; and *their speech shall whisper out of the dust*. (2 Nephi 26:8, 15–16; emphasis added)

CALL TO ACTION: How have the words of the Book of Mormon whispered to you? How has the Book of Mormon better helped you to hear and recognize the voice of God?

Hearing the Covenantal Speech
of King Benjamin

By Taylor Halverson

KING BENJAMIN FAITHFULLY NURTURED HIS people throughout his life. He took seriously God's command to leaders to keep and preserve the scriptures that contains God's covenants, to read the scriptures regularly, and to live and teach these covenantal instructions to others (see Deuteronomy 17:14–20).

As a father, King Benjamin taught his children literacy so they might know how to find, recognize, and hear the voice of God in scripture:

> And he caused that they should be taught in all the language of his fathers, that thereby they might become men of understanding; and that they might know concerning the prophecies which had been spoken by the mouths of their fathers, which were delivered them by the hand of the Lord.
>
> And he also taught them concerning the records which were engraven on the plates of brass, saying: My sons, I

would that ye should remember that
were it not for these plates, which contain
these records and these commandments,
we must have suffered in ignorance,
even at this present time, not knowing
the mysteries of God. (Mosiah 1:2–3)

As parents, teachers, and leaders, we share
King Benjamin's role to teach those in our
stewardship of the things of God, to teach them
to remember God's commandments, and to
teach them from the word of God.

We noted before that the last speech or
dying words of a faithful leader or prophet
should provide a time for us to pause and listen
more closely. King Benjamin's speech is such an
opportunity. He knew that he was growing old.
He knew that he soon must die. He knew that
the peace and prosperity of his people were of
paramount importance. He therefore created
an orderly transition of power of kingship from
himself to his son Mosiah. More importantly,
King Benjamin gathered his people to instruct
them on how to experience thriving lives of joy
centered on Jesus. Teaching the words delivered
to him by an angel, King Benjamin declared,

Behold, I am come to declare unto
you the glad tidings of great joy. . . .
For behold, the time cometh, and
is not far distant, that with power,
the Lord Omnipotent who reigneth,

who was, and is from all eternity to all eternity, shall come down from heaven among the children of men, and shall dwell in a tabernacle of clay, and shall go forth amongst men, working mighty miracles, such as healing the sick, raising the dead, causing the lame to walk, the blind to receive their sight, and the deaf to hear, and curing all manner of diseases. . . .

And he shall be called Jesus Christ, the Son of God, the Father of heaven and earth, the Creator of all things from the beginning; and his mother shall be called Mary.

And lo, he cometh unto his own, that salvation might come unto the children of men even through faith on his name. (Mosiah 3:3, 5, 8–9)

Before King Benjamin delivered this beautiful testimony, he first needed to prepare his people to receive his message. He labored diligently to help them hear the word of God by doing six things.

First, he issued a proclamation inviting everyone to gather to hear him.

Second, he invited everyone to gather at a sacred location—the temple—where they were more likely to be spiritual attuned to hear and receive his message.

Third, he erected a tall tower so that the sound of his voice would carry to the entire congregation.

Fourth, he had the families pitch their tents so they faced toward him, eliminating any physical obstructions to his voice.

Fifth, he wrote his speech so that those who could not hear or who could not attend would later have access to his word. We in the latter-days are beneficiaries of this scribal effort.

Sixth, King Benjamin introduced his stirring speech with a series of loving invitations centered on the theme of hearing:

> My brethren, all ye that have assembled yourselves together, you that can *hear my words* which I shall speak unto you this day; for I have not commanded you to come up hither to trifle with the words which I shall speak, but that you should *hearken* unto me, and *open your ears* that ye may *hear*, and your hearts that ye may understand, and your minds that the mysteries of God may be unfolded to your view. (Mosiah 2:9; emphasis added)

What good is a speech if no one hears? What good is it to speak the truth if listeners do not hearken? King Benjamin pleaded with his people to let the words he had carefully prepared enter their hearts through their ears as seeds of everlasting life.

Throughout his speech, King Benjamin taught the people what truths they should know of God and what they should do to be on the covenant path. At the conclusion of his speech, the people willingly hearkened to King Benjamin, and as a community they joined in a covenant to follow God and His commandments:

> Yea, we believe all the words which thou hast spoken unto us [the people had hearkened]; and also, we know of their surety and truth, because of the Spirit of the Lord Omnipotent, which has wrought a mighty change in us, or in our hearts, that we have no more disposition to do evil, but to do good continually.
>
> . . . we are willing to enter into a covenant with our God to do his will, and to be obedient to his commandments in all things that he shall command us, all the remainder of our days. (Mosiah 5:2, 5)

This is one of the greatest examples in scripture of what it means to *hearken*. We believe in God and are willing to make and keep covenants with Him.

Symbolically, our weekly sacrament service provides an opportunity for us to hearken to the voice of God and to join His covenantal community:

> O God, the Eternal Father, we ask thee in the name of thy Son, Jesus Christ, to bless and sanctify this bread to the souls of all those who partake of it, that they may eat in remembrance of the body of thy Son, and witness unto thee, O God, the Eternal Father, that they are *willing to take upon them the name of thy Son*, and always remember him and keep his commandments which he has given them; that they may always have his Spirit to be with them. Amen. (D&C 20:77; emphasis added)

CALL TO ACTION: As parents, teachers, and leaders, how do we prepare the conditions for others to hear the voice of God? How do we ensure that we are hearing the voice of God so we can teach truth to others?

We Are All Laborers in God's Vineyard

By Taylor Halverson

THE CHURCH OF JESUS CHRIST of Latter-day Saints is organized in a way that gives all of us the opportunity to teach and learn from one another. In this structure, the teacher is no better than the learner, and the learner is no better than the teacher. All are encouraged to pursue understanding of the gospel and to declare our testimony to others.

Our Church culture is a bit like what was found among the Nephites during the time of Alma the Younger. King Mosiah II (the son of King Benjamin) dissolved kingship and instituted a system of judges. Alma the Younger was simultaneously the chief judge and the chief priest in the Nephite community. In Alma 1, Nehor had come among the people preaching a successful false doctrine that all teachers should become popular and be supported by the people. Seeking to enforce his false doctrine by the sword, Nehor killed Gideon. For that crime, Alma pronounced death upon Nehor, according to the Law of Moses.

Soon thereafter, Mormon explained, Nehor's doctrine led to much contention within the Church. Many covenantal members had heard and listened to Nehor and subsequently failed to hearken to the words of their living prophet, Alma. These individuals fell away and caused pain and affliction to those who sought to stay faithful. But the faithful were empowered by God in their patience and suffering. Instead of adopting the false doctrine of Nehor, God's people were willing to hearken to each other and to treat each other with equity:

> And when the priests left their labor to impart the word of God unto the people, the people also left their labors to *hear the word of God.* And when the priest had imparted unto them the word of God they all returned again diligently unto their labors; *and the priest, not esteeming himself above his hearers, for the preacher was no better than the hearer*, neither was the teacher any better than the learner; and thus they were all equal, and they did all labor, every man according to his strength.
>
> And they did impart of their substance, every man according to that which he had, to the poor, and the needy, and the sick, and the afflicted; and they did not wear costly apparel, yet they were neat and comely.

And thus they did establish the affairs of the church; and thus they began to have continual peace again, notwithstanding all their persecutions. (Alma 1:26–28: emphasis added)

This equality of hearing, teaching, and learning led to continual peace.

We have seen wards that have decided not to call permanent adult Sunday school teachers. Instead, as in sacrament meeting where we all receive opportunities to teach the truth, each week a different member of the ward teaches the lessons. In our observation, this has led to a magnification of teaching and learning, because each member recognizes his or her role in contributing to the learning environment. One week one person teaches, and the rest are hearers. The next week, another individual teaches, and the past teachers are now hearers. No one is better than the other. All are edified of all.

There are many ways that such equality of hearing, leading to continual peace, can occur. Each of these require a bit of planning and preparation. In any teaching setting, each person should come ready to hear, receive, share, and participate. Each individual should take turns listening and sharing. No one should dominate the conversation to the exclusion of hearing the voices of others. In families, each individual should have an opportunity to participate and be heard by others from the oldest to the youngest. Even Jesus took time to be with and listen to the "least of these."

CALL TO ACTION: How do you contribute to others hearing the voice of God?

Hearing the Word of God through the Fog of Contention

By Taylor Halverson

KING MOSIAH'S SONS WALKED AWAY from the power, prestige, and worldly pleasures of kingship to empower others to be kings and queens to God, by means of the gospel. These stalwart missionaries spent more than a decade living among those who were seen by their own community of Nephites to be the fear-inducing and debauched Lamanites. Ammon, Aaron, Omner, Himni, and their companions did not hearken to the distracting voices of those around them calling for ignoring— or worse, exterminating—the Lamanites. Instead, these diligent souls hearkened to the persistent call from God that endures even to this day: "Behold, I sent you out to testify and warn the people, and it becometh every man who hath been warned to warn his neighbor" (D&C 88:81).

Ammon is one of the heroes of this story. Turning aside the opportunity to be a prince or a king in his own country, he turned to a life of dangerous service protecting the flocks of an enemy king. Shocked by Ammon's brazen acts of love, service, and courage, King Lamoni of the Lamanites could not contain his inquisitive wonderings as to what would inspire Ammon. As Lamoni listened to the words of Ammon, his heart slowly thawed, and he realized his deep need for accepting Jesus. When he did, he slumped to the earth as though he were dead.

This unusual spectacle caused a commotion among the king's household and among his people. Many gathered, and in the confusing swirl of speculation some threatened murder against Ammon, who had also fallen to the ground overcome with joy. Loyal and faithful Abish, who had previously been converted to God, sought to quell the uprising and took the hand of the fallen king. As a symbolic resurrection, he revived and stood on his feet. Seeing the contention among his people, Lamoni immediately began teaching and testifying of the truths he had learned. What happened next is instructive:

> And he, immediately, seeing the contention among his people, went forth and began to rebuke them, and to teach them the words which he had *heard* from the mouth of Ammon; and as many as *heard* his words believed, and were converted unto the Lord.
>
> But there were many among them who would not *hear* his words; therefore they went their way. (Alma 19:31–32; emphasis added)

The chain of conversion happened because of *hearing the word of God*. Ammon heard those words from his father, Mosiah, and was converted. King Lamoni heard them from Ammon and was converted. And those of Lamoni's people who hearkened to him were also converted and formed the foundation for a righteous community of Lamanites that would endure for generations.

CALL TO ACTION: When there is disagreement, conflict, discouragement, or contention, hearkening to the truths of God can bring order, purpose, peace, and solidarity.

Prayers of Hearing and Gratitude for God Hearing

By Taylor Halverson

SOMETIMES OUR FOCUS NEEDS NOT be on hearing only, but also on expressing our gratitude to God for having heard us in the past. We see such an example in the Book of Mormon. Alma the Younger embarked with other faithful members on a mission among the hard-hearted Nephites. There they encountered the Zoramites, whose gospel focused on self-aggrandizement and pride. In fact, the name *Zoram* may come from the Hebrew words *zo* and *ram*, meaning "he who exalts himself" or "this one is exalted." Furthermore, they created an "exalted" tower called the *Ram*eumptom where they could publicly declare their exaltation.

When the rich and proud Zoramites would not hear nor hearken to Alma, he turned to speak to the lowly and humble among them. Teaching these eager learners who wanted to know better how to recognize the voice of God in their lives, Alma quoted the ancient prophet Zenos's teaching on prayer and worship. We see a significant contrast between the self-aggrandizing prayer of the Zoramites and the soulful supplication of a humble follower of God pleading that He hear them. Our hearing God sometimes comes in the form of God hearing us, hearing our prayers, and answering our needs. As you listen to Zenos, you might ask, "When was the last time I expressed heartfelt gratitude to God for Him *hearing me*?"

> For he said: Thou art merciful, O God, for thou hast *heard* my prayer, even when I was in the wilderness; yea, thou wast merciful when I prayed concerning those who were mine enemies, and thou didst turn them to me.
>
> Yea, O God, and thou wast merciful unto me when I did cry unto thee in my field; when I did cry unto thee in my prayer, and thou didst *hear* me.
>
> And again, O God, when I did turn to my house thou didst *hear* me in my prayer.
>
> And when I did turn unto my closet, O Lord, and prayed unto thee, thou didst *hear* me.
>
> Yea, thou art merciful unto thy children when they cry unto thee, to be *hear*d of thee and not of men, and thou wilt *hear* them.
>
> Yea, O God, thou hast been merciful unto me, and *heard* my cries in the midst of thy congregations.

Yea, and thou hast also *heard* me when I have been cast out and have been despised by mine enemies; yea, thou didst *hear* my cries, and wast angry with mine enemies, and thou didst visit them in thine anger with speedy destruction.

And thou didst *hear* me because of mine afflictions and my sincerity; and *it is because of thy Son that thou hast been thus merciful unto me*, therefore I will cry unto thee in all mine afflictions, for in thee is my joy; for thou hast turned thy judgments away from me, because of thy Son. (Alma 33:4–11; emphasis added)

It is not just our hearing that matters. God is the all-knowing hearer. His hearing matters. We want and need God to hear. God has promised to hear us. God has heard us.

CALL TO ACTION: How has God heard your prayers? What experiences have taught you that God hears and knows your needs?

Hearing the Mild Voice of God

By Taylor Halverson

NEPHI AND LEHI, SONS OF Helaman, took seriously their charge to do good in the world (see Helaman 5:12). They left behind significant security and privileges to spend time with those who would harm them, preaching among the Lamanites in the Land of Nephi. There they were thrown into prison and left to suffer without food as they awaited execution. But when their executioners arrived to commit the foul deed, "Nephi and Lehi were encircled about as if by fire, even insomuch that they durst not lay their hands upon them for fear lest they should be burned" (Helaman 5:23). God had protected His servants.

This incredible experience struck the Lamanites and the Nephite dissenters dumb with amazement, giving Nephi and Lehi an opportunity to testify of God's power. Next, an earthquake forcefully shook the walls and foundation of the prison. Then a darkness enveloped everyone in the prison. And from within the darkness they all unmistakably and undeniably heard a voice declare this simple message: "Repent ye, repent ye, and seek no more to destroy my servants whom I have sent unto you to declare good tidings" (Helaman 5:29).

What is so compelling about this story for teaching about hearing God is that after these incredible experiences of seeing consuming fire not hurt Nephi and Lehi, of feeling a violent earthquake, and of being enveloped by pervasive darkness, the piercing truth of God's mild voice was heard:

> And it came to pass when they heard this voice, and beheld that it was not a voice of thunder, neither was it a voice of a great tumultuous noise, but behold, it was a still voice of perfect mildness, as if it had been a whisper, and it did pierce even to the very soul. (Helaman 5:30)
> Those who had sought the destruction of God's servants heard the voice of God and immediately began to repent and to call upon the voice. As they did, the power of the Holy Ghost washed over them. And then, "[I]t came to pass that there came a voice unto them, yea, a pleasant voice, as if it were a whisper, saying: Peace, peace be unto you, because of your faith in my Well Beloved, who was from the foundation of the world" (Helaman 5:46–47).

We shouldn't need and we definitely shouldn't wait for God to wake us up with an earthquake before we hear Him. We can turn our spiritual ears to hear His soothingly mild voice of gentle rebuke and love.

CALL TO ACTION: When has God used your life experiences to help you hear Him?

Hearing the Voice of God Is to See that All Things Testify of His Son

By Taylor Halverson

AS THE BOOK OF MORMON narrative progresses through time, we see the discouraging cycles of pride and wickedness that disrupt the peace and prosperity of the people. Throughout the record, we see that God lovingly called out to His people to hear His voice by sending prophets to teach and testify that salvation and peace is in and only through Jesus Christ.

When the former chief judge and prophet Nephi publicly called on the corrupt judges and leaders to cease from their twisted ways, they clamored for the people to anger against Nephi. But some in the audience had listened with open hearts. They silenced the judges and urged Nephi to continue his message. Seeking to show that he was not alone in his testimony, Nephi reviewed the some of the words and deeds of former prophets of whom all his listeners would have known: Abraham, Moses,

Zenos, Zenock, Ezias, Isaiah, Jeremiah, Lehi (who left Jerusalem), and Nephi (son of Lehi).

Nephi focused his message on the undeniable truth that God was with all these prophets and that all that they taught and did was to point people to Jesus Christ. With this powerful cloud of witnesses, Nephi then boldly declared this message:

> And also almost *all of our fathers*, even down to this time; yea, they *have testified of the coming of Christ*, and have looked forward, and have rejoiced in his day which is to come.
>
> And behold, he is God, and he is with them, and he did manifest himself unto them, that they were redeemed by him; and they gave unto him glory, because of that which is to come. (Helaman 8:22–23; emphasis added)

We hear God as we see Jesus in the messages of the prophets. And we hear God by seeing and acknowledging His mighty acts and miracles on our behalf.

Nephi further taught us that priesthood powers, duties, and responsibilities are a way to hear God's voice in our lives:

> Yea, and behold I say unto you, that Abraham not only knew of

these things [i.e., the coming of Jesus Christ], but there were many before the days of Abraham who were *called by the order of God*; yea, even after the order of his Son; and this that it should be *shown unto the people*, a great many thousand years before his coming, that even *redemption should come unto them*. (Helaman 8:18; emphasis added)

God acts through priesthood power, and He delegates His power through the priesthood as a way of teaching His people about salvation. Seeing, receiving, acting on, and honoring the priesthood is a way of hearing the voice of God in our lives.

CALL TO ACTION: What evidence for God's love do you see in His creations? In His power?

Hearing Jesus Christ

By Taylor Halverson

WHEN JESUS CAME TO VISIT His people in the New World, they received the treasured gift of several days of direct interaction with Him. They were able to see Him. They were blessed to touch Him and to be touched by Him. And they *heard* Him! He spoke to them at length across several days. Though the record does not retain the details, it seems as though the audience was transfixed in reverence as Jesus spoke so that there was little to no distraction from hearing Him.

After delivering a reprise of the Sermon on the Mount and teaching the core doctrines of salvation (see 3 Nephi 12–16), Jesus paused to take in the scene. He knew that there was much for them to ponder and process, and He told them, "I perceive that ye are weak, that ye cannot understand all my words which I am commanded of the Father to speak unto you at this time" (3 Nephi 17:2). But the people did not want to leave Jesus. They wanted to hear more from Him. They wanted to linger:

> And it came to pass that when Jesus had thus spoken, he cast his eyes round about again on the multitude,

and beheld they were in tears, and did look steadfastly upon him as if they would ask him to tarry a little longer with them. (3 Nephi 17:5)

Jesus, the God of love and mercy, could not restrain Himself from such expressions of devout attention. He declared to the people, "Behold, my bowels are filled with compassion towards you" (3 Nephi 17:6). He tarried a while longer to be with the people and to teach them through acts of compassionate healing and prayer. Being with Jesus is to hear God.

CALL TO ACTION: When you have time with God, do you petition Him to tarry longer with you? What else have you learned by spending more time listening to God?

God Wants to Hear Us.

Have We Heard Him?

By Taylor Halverson

ONE OF THE SAD TRUTHS seen repeatedly throughout the Book of Mormon is that God's children often forget to call upon Him, even though God stands ready and willing to hear us so that we can hear Him! Mormon lamented this state of his society after spending years declaring the truth of God's loving mercy to them:

> But behold, I was without hope, for I knew the judgments of the Lord which should come upon them; for they repented not of their iniquities, but did *struggle for their lives without calling upon that Being who created them.* (Mormon 5:2; emphasis added)

Imagine a parent watching a child stuck struggling with a difficult task. That parent stands ready and willing to lend assistance and support. Imagine if the child refuses to ask. Or the child refuses to acknowledge that assistance is available while languishing in despair and suffering. Sure, struggle and effort are required for growth and development. But all of us need help, support, and encouragement in our difficulties. None of us can find enduring joy in this life if we act as though we are entirely independent from anyone and everything. God wants us to hear His loving voice of kindness and support. But we must ask for it. He wants to hear us so that we can hear Him.

We see this same pattern during the life of the brother of Jared. After God led His people forth from the Tower of Babel with mighty acts of salvation, the brother of Jared forgot to call upon God for more than four years! God eventually intervened:

> And it came to pass at the end of four years that the Lord came again unto the brother of Jared, and stood in a cloud and talked with him. And for the space of three hours did *the Lord talk with the brother of Jared, and chastened him because he remembered not to call upon the name of the Lord.*
>
> And the brother of Jared repented of the evil which he had done, and *did call upon the name of the Lord* for his brethren who were with him. And the Lord said unto him: I will forgive thee and thy brethren of their sins; but thou shalt not sin any more, for ye shall remember that my Spirit will not always strive with man; wherefore,

> if ye will sin until ye are fully ripe ye shall be cut off from the presence of the Lord. And these are my thoughts upon the land which I shall give you for your inheritance; for it shall be a land choice above all other lands. (Ether 2:14–15; emphasis added)

God makes it abundantly clear in this revelation to the brother of Jared that *we cannot prosper* if we do not call upon God. We must allow God to hear us. When we do, we are more likely to hear Him and experience the prospering promises reserved for us, just like the brother of Jared experienced when he first called upon God before leaving the Tower of Babel. In fact, the brother of Jared cried unto the Lord three times. And three times the brother of Jared heard the voice of the Lord speak compassion and promises to him:

> And it came to pass that the brother of Jared did *cry unto the Lord*, and *the Lord had compassion* upon Jared. . . .
> And it came to pass that the brother of Jared did *cry unto the Lord*, and *the Lord had compassion* upon their friends and their families. . . .
> And it came to pass that the brother of Jared did *cry unto the Lord* according to that which had been spoken by the mouth of Jared.

And it came to pass that *the Lord did hear* the brother of Jared, *and had compassion* upon him. (Ether 1:35, 37, 39–40; emphasis added.)

God stands ready to pour out His immeasurable compassion upon us. We can hear Him. We need only to ask Him to hear us!

CALL TO ACTION: Plan daily time to call upon God; prepare yourself to listen and record what you hear from Him.

The Restoration of All Things Began with the Command to Hear Him!

By Taylor Halverson

THE BURSTING OPEN OF THE heavens began on a beautiful spring day in upstate New York in 1820. Joseph Smith, concerned for the welfare of his soul and genuinely perplexed at the competing truth claims advocated on all sides, ventured forth into the woods to ask the One and True Source that he knew he could trust with complete confidence.

The manner of having his prayer answered was wholly unexpected. Joseph narrates,

> I saw a pillar of light exactly over my head, above the brightness of the sun, which descended gradually until it fell upon me. . . .
> When the light rested upon me I saw two Personages, whose brightness and glory defy all description, standing above me in the air. One of them spake unto me, calling

me by name and said, pointing to the other—*This is My Beloved Son. Hear Him!* (Joseph Smith—History 1:16–17)

Three marvelous truths are packed into this testimony from Joseph Smith.

First, *God the Father knows us by name!*

Of all the things that God the Father could have said, He began with the most intimate and loving of words: Joseph's own name. God is the father of all. He knows each of us, by name! When you pray, listen to Him. Do you hear Him calling you by name?

Second, *God the Father commands us to hear His Son.*

The creator of the universe—who holds life and death in His hands; who sees past, present, and future; who knows all things that ever were, are, or will be—did not dominate the stage, did not speak endlessly of everything He knew and loved. Instead, in simple humility He asked Joseph Smith, and by extension all of us, to hear the Son.

Third, *hearing is the foundation of the Restoration.*

At the founding of the Restoration, God the Father did not tell us to "watch" Jesus or to "follow" Jesus or "see Jesus," even though each of those activities is necessary and needful on our covenant path. God's first command of the Restoration was to *hear*! We are to hear and follow Jesus in all things. If we want to know the key to unlocking the Restoration and our salvation, we should look no further than God's timeless command to *hear Him*.

CALL TO ACTION: Review the story of the First Vision and ponder again what we learn from God's command to *Hear Him!*

Hearing God in Being Called to Serve

By Taylor Halverson

HAVE YOU EVER THOUGHT ABOUT the word we use throughout the Church to describe official responsibilities to serve God and His people? We receive a *call to serve*. We receive *callings*!

Why do we use such language? Because God calls to us, He speaks to us, and in that speaking He invites us to act in some capacity to serve and love others. When we are humble, we *hear the voice of God*; we hear His call for us to follow the example of His Son Jesus Christ to give of our time, talent, and lives in the loving service of others.

We don't assign ourselves service opportunities. On our own, we do not put ourselves into positions or assume responsibilities. Instead, we are part of a larger, cohesive, whole body that works together for the larger purposes of God. We are called by the voice of God to serve where He would have us, for a season.

If we wish to hearken to the voice of God more fully in our lives, humbling and willingly accepting divinely revealed callings is one way to accomplish that righteous desire.

CALL TO ACTION: How do you hear the voice of God in your calling?

Conclusion

Hear Him! That directive is one of the consistent themes preserved in scripture. The scriptures are themselves evidence of those who have heard God and recorded His words so that later generations would benefit. That preserved wisdom to hear God echoes throughout the centuries and is as relevant in our day as in times past.

Hear Him! This is one of the great invitations of our lives. God the Father has consistently commanded us to hear His Son Jesus Christ. As we have demonstrated in this book, a careful review of the times when the words of God the Father have been recorded, these words have focused our attention on His Son—on hearing Him.

Hear Him! God's voice can be found everywhere in our lives. We find it in the cracks of conversations, in the breaking forth of sunlight at the dawning day, in the quiet moments of wondering, in the marvelous gifts of our physical bodies, at the intersection of our relations with loved ones, and in the expansive nature of God's Spirit that is ever ready to shed joy into our hearts as we fulfill our covenantal promise to always remember the Son.

Search your heart. Remember the times when you have heard God, felt His love, experienced

His atoning power. Take courage that you can and will hear Him as you seek. Remember to be diligent, patient, and persistent. By small means are great things brought to pass.

Each day, make time to listen to God in the scriptures, in prayer, in your heart, in your life, in the lives of those around you, and in the beautiful created order God has provided us as we participate in the plan of salvation. Schedule time to review the words of living prophets. Make time to regularly document how you have heard God in your life. Actively share your testimony of hearing God with others. Fortify the faith of others as they seek to hear Him.

As you do these things your heart will be strengthened, your love will wax bold in the presence of God, and you will feel more fully the sure promise of His love in your life.

Appendix A:
Words and Concepts to Look for in Scripture and in Your Life to Hear the Voice of God

There are many words throughout scripture that may prompt us to listen more carefully, to hear more fully with open hearts, and to heed more diligently. Use the list below as a starting point for words and phrases to look for in your scripture study on the topic of *Hear Him*.

- Hear
- Hearken
- Listen
- Call and Calling
- Pray and prayer
- Heed
- Obey
- Cry and cry out
- Bid and bidding
- Command
- Sing and song
- Arouse and awaken
- Proclaim
- Ask
- Invoke
- Address

- Declare
- Summon
- Decree
- Prophesy
- Hark
- Perceive
- Publish
- Tell
- Understand
- Witness
- Behold

Appendix B:
Ten Simple Ways to Better Hear the Voice of God in Your Life

THERE ARE SO MANY POWERFUL and profound ways to *hear Him!* If you are looking to jump-start your spiritual listening, try any of these ten suggestions.

1. Plan time to be with God.
2. Minimize distractions in your life (TV, internet, radio, phone, electronics, and so on).
3. Daily read or listen to His words searchingly, with a purpose or a specific question in mind.
4. Pray and talk to God with a purpose or a specific question.
5. Listen to God (be ready with pen and paper).
6. Record the impressions you receive from God.
7. Make plans to act on impressions you receive.
8. Reflect on and record what you've learned by acting on impressions from God.
9. Learn from others how they experience God's voice in their lives.

10. Experiment on the word of God and experiment with various ways to hear the voice of God.

About the Authors

Taylor and Lisa Halverson

Taylor David Halverson

TAYLOR HALVERSON IS AN ASPIRING master learner and an Entrepreneurship Professor in the BYU Marriott School of Business. He has discovered his life purpose to help people *find* and *act* on the *best ideas* and *tools* in order to *experience enduring joy*.

As an executive coach and entrepreneur, Taylor builds leaders and businesses while creating transformative professional and personal development experiences.

Taylor leads acclaimed travel tours to incredible locations throughout the world (Israel, China, India, Europe, Central America, and America's National Parks). Tour members have loved his irresistible enthusiasm, encyclopedic knowledge, spirit of adventure, and sense of fun.

Taylor is a prolific author and editor of twenty books and more than three hundred articles and a developer of breakthrough scripture study resources with Book of Mormon Central (ScripturePlus app & Come, Follow Me Insights videos with Tyler Griffin) and BYU's Virtual Scripture Group (3D Ancient Jerusalem project).

Taylor lives in Springville, Utah, with his wife Lisa and their two kids. He loves to spend time with his family on all sorts of adventures including exploring the nooks and crannies of the American West and Southwest, participating with geology and archaeology teams on location, creating and mixing electronic music, watching and discussing edifying shows, reading good books, playing games, learning, and laughing.

Taylor's academic training includes:

- BA, Ancient Near Eastern Studies, Brigham Young University
- MA, Biblical Studies, Yale University
- MS, Instructional Systems Technology, Indiana University
- PhD, Instructional Systems Technology, Indiana University
- PhD, Judaism & Christianity in Antiquity, Indiana University

Learn more at taylorhalverson.com.

Would you like to join Taylor's email list? Do so and receive a free humorous ebook called the *Memoirs of The Ward Rumor Control Coordinator*: shorturl.at/koqO5.

Lisa Maren Rampton Halverson

An Oregonian by birth and temperament, Lisa Halverson is beginning to love the arid American Southwest which she now calls home with her husband and two children (adoption miracles!).

Lisa studied International Relations (BA) and Modern Jewish and Middle Eastern history (MA) at Stanford University (Go Cardinals!), then taught high school English for ten years. She holds a PhD in Instructional Psychology & Technology from Brigham Young University (Go Cougars!) and now teaches for two universities. She is a senior director of a nonprofit devoted to increasing women's participation in and voices for ethical government.

Tyler Jay Griffin

TYLER J. GRIFFIN WAS BORN and raised in Providence, Utah, in the beautiful Cache Valley. After serving in the Brazil Curitiba Mission, he returned home and married an angel named Kiplin Crook. They have ten children (five boys and five girls). They love spending time in the mountains, playing board games, doing house projects, and being together. He and his wife also enjoy leading tours to biblical sites.

Tyler's bachelor's degree was in electrical engineering, and his master's and doctorate degrees are both in instructional technology. Tyler began his career by teaching seminary for six years in Brigham City, Utah. He spent the next seven years teaching at the Logan Institute of Religion adjacent to Utah State University. He has taught at Brigham Young University since August 2010.

He is a cofounder of BYU Virtual Scriptures Group, which develops digital learning resources to enhance scriptural immersion and understanding.

He authored *When Heaven Feels Distant*; coauthored *Come Unto Me: Illuminating the Savior's Life, Mission, Parables, and Miracles*; and coedited *Millions Shall Know Brother Joseph Again*. Tyler enjoys presenting at BYU Education Week, firesides, and conferences.

Other Books by Taylor Halverson

History of Creativity in the Arts, Science, and Technology: Pre-History to 1500, 3rd edition (with Brent Strong and Mark Davis)

History of Creativity in the Arts, Science, and Technology: 1500 to Present, 3rd edition (with Brent Strong and Mark Davis)

Finding Myself Alone: Positive Insights, Thoughts, and Discoveries from LDS Singles (edited with Mike Agrelius)

Millions Shall Know Brother Joseph Again: Daily Inspiration from the Prophet Joseph Smith (with Tyler Griffin)

Letters from a Christmas Elf: Unexpected Humor for Any Season (with Kirsten Johnston and Kurt Johnston)

Memoirs of the Ward Rumor Control Coordinator (with Richard Halverson)

Distance Education Innovations and New Learning Environments: Combining Traditional Teaching Methods and Emerging Technologies

Learning for Eternity: Best BYU Speeches and Articles on Learners and Learning (with Brad Wilcox and Lisa Halverson, forthcoming)